YORK NOTES

General Editors: Professor A.N. Jeffares (*University of Stirling*) & Professor Suheil Bushrui (*American University of Beirut*)

Tom Stoppard

ROSENCRANTZ AND GUILDENSTERN ARE DEAD

Notes by P. H. Parry
BA (BRISTOL) MA (BIRMINGHAM) PH D (ST ANDREWS)
Lecturer in English, University of St Andrews

LONGMAN
YORK PRESS

YORK PRESS
Immeuble Esseily, Place Riad Solh, Beirut.

LONGMAN GROUP LIMITED
Longman House,
Burnt Mill,
Harlow,
Essex.

First published 1984
Second impression 1986
ISBN 0 582 79218 5
Produced by Longman Group (FE) Ltd
Printed in Hong Kong

Contents

Part 1

Introduction

Tom Stoppard

Tom Stoppard was born in Czechoslovakia in 1937, the younger son of Eugene Straussler, a doctor employed by a leading shoe company. Two years later the family moved to Singapore, and from there, in order to escape the Japanese invasion, Mrs Straussler and her sons were evacuated to India. Dr Straussler, who stayed behind, was killed. In 1946 Mrs Straussler married Kenneth Stoppard, who was serving with the British army in India. The Stoppards moved to England where Tom continued his education. From 1954 to 1963 he worked as a journalist, first for two West of England newspapers and then as a freelance.*

Although *Rosencrantz and Guildenstern are Dead* (1966) was Stoppard's first major success, he had already tried his hand as a dramatist by writing plays for both television and radio; he has continued to write for both these media, often producing work of the highest quality. In 1966 he published a novel, *Lord Malquist and Mr Moon*, which in its interests and imagery is clearly a close cousin to his early plays.

Stoppard is now firmly established, on the strength of *Rosencrantz and Guildenstern are Dead*, *The Real Inspector Hound* (1968), *Jumpers* (1972), and *Travesties* (1974), as a dramatist of wit, inventiveness, and technical brilliance. All of these plays, as he has himself recognised, are broadly similar in structure and reveal the same concerns (with, for example, the physical nature of the stage, and with stage illusion). Rather than repeat these early successes indefinitely Stoppard has recently sought, taking the lead from his portrait of Lenin in *Travesties* and prompted by what he saw and heard during a visit to Czechoslovakia in 1977, to treat overtly political themes from the vantage-point of an expatriate East European dramatist sympathetic towards the sufferings of dissidents (including dissident dramatists) in Eastern Europe. *Every Good Boy Deserves Favour* (1979), *Professional Foul* (1979), and *Dogg's Hamlet, Cahoot's Macbeth* (1979) are all, in their

*Stoppard's entry in *Who's Who* provides a basic outline of his career. Reference should also be made to: Ronald Hayman, *Tom Stoppard*, Heinemann Educational, London, 1977 (third edition, revised and expanded, 1979); Jim Hunter, *Tom Stoppard's Plays*, Faber & Faber, London, 1982; Felicia Hardison Londré, *Tom Stoppard*, Frederick Ungar, New York, 1981.

very different ways, examples of this new political explicitness. (The last-named is a pair of linked plays. The strange second half of the title is an allusion to the Czechoslovak playwright Pavel Kohout who, prevented by the authorities from staging plays in public, has adapted Shakespeare's *Macbeth* for performance in private homes. In English slang 'to be in cahoots' with someone is to be in collusion with him: thus Stoppard punningly suggests both the name of the dissident playwright and the atmosphere of secrecy and confidential co-operation in which he is forced to perform.) *Night and Day* (1978), though its setting is Africa, is similarly explicit in its political reference; in it Stoppard has drawn on his experience as a journalist in order to produce a serious discussion of press freedom. Despite its elaborate stage-set and its harking back to earlier work,* *Night and Day* is much closer to the standard 'well-made play' than anything else that he has yet written.

Stoppard, as will surprise no one who remembers his habit of grafting so much of his best work on to plays that are well established in the standard repertory, has also proved himself a spirited adaptor of foreign plays. *Undiscovered Country* (1979) is his version of a play by Arthur Schnitzler (1862–1931), the Austrian dramatist and controversial man of letters. *On the Razzle* (1981) is a reworking of another Austrian play, this time by Johann Nestroy (1801–62).

Literary background: Shakespeare's *Hamlet*

William Shakespeare (1564–1616) is the single greatest influence on *Rosencrantz and Guildenstern are Dead.* Without, at the very least, an elementary knowledge of Shakespeare's *The Tragedy of Hamlet, Prince of Denmark* (*c.* 1601) Stoppard's play cannot be understood.

In broadest outline *Hamlet* is the story of two brothers (one dead, the other living), of the woman who is wife to both, and of her son. Hamlet, king of Denmark, is murdered by his brother (Claudius) who marries his widow (Gertrude) and ascends his throne. Prince Hamlet, son of King Hamlet and Gertrude, is sickened by his mother's incest. (The marriage of a woman to her deceased husband's brother was considered to be incestuous in Shakespeare's England.) His father's ghost informs Hamlet of the murder and commands him to exact vengeance on Claudius without harming Gertrude. The rest of the play, the longest that Shakespeare wrote, is an intricate and in places obscure battle of wits between Claudius and Hamlet, in which Claudius tries to discover his nephew's intentions, while Hamlet seeks first to prove his uncle's

*In *Albert's Bridge* (1967) Albert sings a broken version of 'Night and Day', a popular song that provides both title and underlying symbolism for Stoppard's later play. Cross-references of this sort abound in Stoppard's work, as they do in the work of Thomas Stearns Eliot (1888–1965) to whom Stoppard has acknowledged an indebtedness.

guilt and then to punish him at the right moment and in a fitting manner.

Something more detailed than a broad outline is required if we are to judge properly the use which Stoppard has made of Shakespeare's text. In the following summary of *Hamlet* italicisation indicates those parts of Shakespeare's play in which Rosencrantz and Guildenstern appear.

Throughout the present work reference is made to, and quotations are taken from, the new Arden edition of *Hamlet*, edited by Harold Jenkins, Methuen, London and New York, 1982. The Arden edition is very full and goes beyond the needs of all save the most advanced students. Other, less elaborate editions include: *Hamlet*, edited by George Rylands, The New Clarendon Shakespeare, Clarendon Press, Oxford, 1947 (and frequently reprinted); and the New Penguin Shakespeare edition, edited by T. J. B. Spencer and with an introduction by Anne Barton, Penguin Books, Harmondsworth, 1980. Students who require step-by-step guidance of an elementary sort through the difficulties of Shakespeare's language may find helpful the New Swan Shakespeare (Advanced Series) edition, edited by Bernard Lott, Longman, London, 1969.

Act 1

Officers of the watch, together with Horatio, Hamlet's close friend, meet at midnight outside the castle of Elsinore to discuss a spectral appearance that has twice been witnessed. Horatio thinks the witnesses mistaken, but before discussion is far advanced the ghost, who looks like the late king, enters. He refuses to speak to them, and they leave in order to summon Hamlet. (I. 2) Claudius is seen despatching various affairs of state. He takes action to stave off a threatened invasion by Fortinbras, son of King Fortinbras of Norway who was killed in battle by Hamlet's father, in the year of young Hamlet's birth. Claudius greets Laertes, who is the son of Polonius, his chief minister, and then by means of hearty commonplaces seeks to reconcile Hamlet to his father's death, his uncle's rule, and his mother's remarriage. Claudius leaves satisfied that he has succeeded, though Hamlet's soliloquy which follows makes it clear to the audience that he has not. News is brought to Hamlet of the spectral appearance which he prepares to encounter at the next midnight. (I. 3) Laertes, who has come from France to attend Claudius's coronation, is about to return. He warns Ophelia, his sister, against placing trust in Hamlet's declarations of love, since, as heir to the throne, he is unlikely to be allowed to marry as he chooses. Polonius repeats the advice with all of the wordiness that is the mark of his character. (I. 4) Hamlet sees the ghost, follows it, and (I. 5) engages it in conversation. The ghost declares itself to be indeed the spirit of the late king, murdered by Claudius. It charges Hamlet to revenge the murder without in any way harming Gertrude. Hamlet agrees, returns to his companions, whom he swears to secrecy, telling them that he may, in order to further his plans, assume a disguise of madness or eccentricity (the famous 'antic disposition' upon which so much discussion has centred).

Act 2

Ophelia tells her father of Hamlet's distraught behaviour. Polonius hurries off to tell Claudius. (II. 2) *Rosencrantz and Guildenstern, childhood companions of the prince, have been hurriedly summoned by Claudius who asks them to discover the cause of Hamlet's strange conduct.* Polonius tells Claudius that Hamlet's madness has been caused by Ophelia's rejection of him and invites Claudius to eavesdrop on Hamlet's next conversation with her. All, save Polonius, leave the stage. Hamlet enters and has a riddling exchange with Polonius, which convinces the latter of the correctness of his diagnosis. He then leaves, *and Rosencrantz and Guildenstern enter, in obedience to Claudius's request. In the conversation that follows Hamlet gets the better of them, learns that they have been sent for, and in return tells them nothing. They announce the imminent arrival of a troupe of travelling players just as Polonius hurries on stage to make the same announcement. Hamlet arranges for the players to include in their own performance a speech of his own composing. Once Rosencrantz and Guildenstern have left,* Hamlet announces in soliloquy his plan of proving the king's guilt by means of a dramatic surprise.

Act 3

Rosencrantz and Guildenstern report their lack of success to Claudius, who determines to spy on the next meeting between Hamlet and Ophelia. He exits in order to do so. Hamlet enters, speaks his most famous soliloquy ('To be, or not to be'), and, upon meeting Ophelia, speaks distractedly to her. Claudius, who overhears him, thinks that his madness is politically dangerous rather than the consequence of unrequited love, and decides to pack him off to England. (III. 2) Hamlet plans his exposure of Claudius: *Rosencrantz and Guildenstern are sent to fetch the players*; Horatio is instructed to watch Claudius carefully. The court assembles to watch the play. Claudius's murder of King Hamlet is enacted in dumb-show and is then repeated in a spoken version. Seeing his crime thus represented, and realising that Hamlet is threatening him, Claudius hurriedly rushes off-stage, calling for lights. *Rosencrantz and Guildenstern are once more sent by Claudius to test Hamlet's madness and to plumb his intentions. Once again they fail.* Polonius tells Hamlet that his mother, Gertrude, wishes to speak to him. (III. 3) *Claudius tells Rosencrantz and Guildenstern that they must accompany Hamlet on his voyage to England.* Polonius decides to hide behind a tapestry in Gertrude's apartments so that he can overhear her interview with Hamlet. Claudius, frightened and conscience-stricken, tries to pray. Hamlet sees him and decides to kill him, but is deterred by the thought that Claudius's soul will be saved from damnation if he is killed at prayer. For this reason Hamlet spares him. Claudius, unaware of the great danger that he has so narrowly escaped, declares that his attempt at prayer has been unsuccessful. (III. 4) Hamlet visits his mother. His conversation frightens her, and when she calls out, Polonius, hidden behind the tapestry, is mistaken by Hamlet for Claudius and is killed. Hamlet tries to convince his mother that her actions are wicked, and appears to be succeeding. At this point the ghost, visible only to Hamlet, enters. Hamlet's conversation with it is interpreted by Gertrude as evidence of his insanity. *The scene ends with Hamlet's declaring his distrust of Rosencrantz and Guildenstern* ('my two schoolfellows, /Whom I will trust as I will adders fang'd') *and his determination to watch them carefully on his voyage to England.*

Act 4

Gertrude tells Claudius of Hamlet's actions. *Claudius sends Rosencrantz and Guildenstern to recover Polonius's body and convey it to the chapel.* (IV. 2) *This they attempt to do, but fail.* (IV. 3) *They bring Hamlet to Claudius.* Hamlet tells him where Polonius's body is to be found, *and is told that he is to voyage to England, attended by Rosencrantz and Guildenstern.* In an aside Claudius lets the audience know that he intends to have Hamlet killed in England. (IV. 4) Hamlet, *accompanied by Rosencrantz and Guildenstern*, watches Fortinbras and his troops passing through Denmark on their way to attack Poland. He reflects on Fortinbras's ability to act in a crisis, superior to his own. (IV. 5) Ophelia is driven mad by Hamlet's treatment of her and by her father's death. Laertes returns to exact vengeance for Polonius's murder. (IV. 6) Hamlet sends a letter to Horatio, telling him of what happened during his voyage to England. The ship carrying him there was attacked by pirates with whom he has joined forces. (IV. 7) Claudius tells Laertes of the part that Hamlet has played in his father's death and Ophelia's madness. News being brought of Hamlet's unexpected return, Claudius and Laertes plot his death. Laertes is to challenge him to a fencing match but is to equip himself with a poisoned blade. Gertrude tells them both that the grief-stricken Ophelia has killed herself.

Act 5

Hamlet meets a gravedigger at his work, and exchanges jests with him. The corpse of Ophelia is brought in for burial. Hamlet and Laertes engage in an unseemly fight in her grave, an incident which stiffens Claudius's resolve to have Hamlet killed. (V. 2) Hamlet tells Horatio how, *suspecting that the sealed orders which Rosencrantz and Guildenstern carried bore him no good, he contrived to open the orders secretly, and change them so as to bring about the deaths of his former schoolfellows. He expresses no remorse over their deaths* ('Why, man, they did make love to this employment;/They are not near my conscience'). News is brought of Laertes's challenge, which Hamlet accepts. In order to ensure that Hamlet is killed he is given a blunted foil; Laertes is given one which has been dipped in poison; and Claudius poisons a cup of wine from which he expects Hamlet to drink. During the excitement of the contest Gertrude, ignorant of what has happened, drinks from the cup. Laertes wounds Hamlet, but is himself wounded by his own blade. He tells Hamlet of the death that awaits them both. Hamlet, at last stirred into action, kills Claudius. The play ends with the arrival of the ambassadors from England, anxious to tell Claudius that his orders (which they do not know that Hamlet has changed) are carried out, and that *Rosencrantz and Guildenstern are dead.* Fortinbras, who has accompanied the ambassadors onto the stage, views the general carnage, claims Denmark as his own, and orders that Hamlet be buried with full military honours.

A note on the text

During the period from May to October in 1964 Stoppard attended a course for young dramatists, held in Berlin and sponsored by the Ford Foundation. One of his contributions to the course was a one-act Shakespeare burlesque *Rosencrantz and Guildenstern meet King Lear* (a style of title modelled on American comedy films of the 1940s and 1950s). Though one of the course assessors thought the work 'a lot of academic twaddle',* Stoppard kept the piece by him. Extended and refined, with King Lear removed, and with a change of title, *Rosencrantz and Guildenstern are Dead* was performed at the Edinburgh Festival

*The assessor was Charles Marowitz who discusses the occasion in his *Confessions of a Counterfeit Critic*, Eyre Methuen, London, 1973, p. 123. Marowitz incorrectly places Stoppard's visit in the summer of 1965, some months after the first performance (in January 1965, also in Berlin) of Marowitz's own version of *Hamlet*. See also Charles Marowitz, *The Marowitz Shakespeare*, Marion Boyars, London, 1978; and Part 3 of these Notes.

Fringe in 1966.* The interest which it aroused there was so great that the National Theatre offered to stage it, and did so in April 1967 in a slightly modified version.

In May 1967 the London publishing house Faber & Faber published the play, in a text which reproduced in the main that of the National Theatre's April production. In 1968 the same publishers brought out a revised version of the play containing numerous minor changes and a different ending. This 1968 version, though strictly a separate edition, is frequently listed in library catalogues as if it were merely a reprint of the 1967 text.

The notes in the present volume follow the 1968 text (the only text with which readers today are likely to be acquainted or which they are likely to see performed) though from time to time reference is also made to the 1967 version.

*The Fringe is the semi-official adjunct to the annual Edinburgh Festival. See Alistair Moffat, *The Edinburgh Fringe*, Johnston & Bacon, London and Edinburgh, 1978, pp. 71–2 for a description of the first performance of Stoppard's play and for extracts (not always favourable) from the reviews.

Part 2

Summaries
of ROSENCRANTZ AND GUILDENSTERN ARE DEAD

A general summary

Rosencrantz and Guildenstern are instructed to report to Claudius, king of Denmark, by a messenger who rouses them from their beds by his fierce banging upon their shutters. On their way towards the court they meet a group of down-at-heel actors who are also travelling to the court where they hope to entertain the royal party.

Claudius tells Rosencrantz and Guildenstern that they are to watch his nephew, the young Prince Hamlet, carefully and are to try to find out why he is behaving in a strange and threatening manner. This task they undertake with commendable persistency but without enthusiasm, skill, or success; events move rapidly and are beyond their control. The entertainment, rewritten for the actors at Hamlet's insistence, both outrages and frightens the king, who is further alarmed by Hamlet's killing of Polonius, one of the principal royal advisors. Claudius sends Rosencrantz and Guildenstern to bring Hamlet to him and decides that they should accompany Hamlet to England bearing sealed orders that will bring about his death.

In part Claudius's plans succeed. Hamlet is put on board ship with Rosencrantz and Guildenstern as companions. They unseal their orders and learn that Hamlet is to be killed but do nothing to warn him. He, in his turn, secretly alters the wording of their orders so as to bring about their deaths. Then, during a pirate attack, Hamlet escapes, leaving Rosencrantz and Guildenstern to travel alone to England and to their fated end.

Detailed summaries

Act 1 (pages 7–12)

Rosencrantz and Guildenstern sit spinning coins and betting on the result. Rosencrantz calls 'heads' more than ninety times, and each time wins the bet. Guildenstern is greatly puzzled by what is going on, while Rosencrantz is largely unconcerned and uncomprehending.

NOTES AND GLOSSARY:

sticks and all: (*colloquial*) sticks and everything else that is appropriate

Seventy-six love: Rosencrantz has won seventy-six times; Guildenstern has not won at all. *Love* (a corruption of French *l'oeuf*, 'the egg') is a term used in tennis scoring to indicate nought. Stoppard's rapid question-and-answer dialogue, which lends itself to analogies drawn from tennis, is derived from similar dialogue in Samuel Beckett's *Waiting for Godot.** Compare the following words in Beckett's play, spoken by Vladimir: 'Come on, Gogo, return the ball, can't you, once in a way?'

The law of probability: which would lead us to expect that, in an extended series of bets, the coins would be likely to come up tails as often as they do heads

***examining the confines of the stage*:** this stage-direction, the significance of the wording of which would be lost in performance, nevertheless alerts the *reader* to one of the play's themes

six monkeys: Guildenstern, who fancies himself as a bit of a philosopher, alludes to a humorous illustration of the belief that the most complicated physical structures can be built up on the hit-or-miss principle provided that the principle is allowed to operate over vast spans of time. If six monkeys are seated in front of six typewriters they will eventually, by a merely random process of pressing keys, produce a text identical to that contained in the complete works of Shakespeare. Vast spans of time may be required because the monkeys will also produce many millions of millions of copies that will differ, sometimes massively and sometimes minutely, from the text of Shakespeare's works

Game?: Rosencrantz asks: 'Have I won the game?'. Guildenstern interprets him as asking: 'Were the monkeys game [that is, sexually willing]?'

rewarding speculation, in either sense: 'speculation' means (a) an interesting line of thought, and (b) a financially profitable deal

law of diminishing returns: a law which states that the first item that makes good a lack is more welcome than the second, the second more welcome than the third,

*Samuel Beckett was born in Dublin (1906) but has for many years lived in Paris. He writes with equal distinction in both French and English. *En attendant Godot* (1952), translated into English by Beckett himself, is a major influence upon *Rosencrantz and Guildenstern are Dead*. See Part 4 of these Notes, pp. 55–6.

and so on. Thus, when one is thirsty, the first glass of water is more welcome than the tenth, and the hundredth is not welcome at all

You spun them yourself: Rosencrantz seeks to counter a charge of unfair play. It is not the possibility of being cheated, however, that is pressing upon Guildenstern's mind

Is *that* what you imagine?: Rosencrantz uses the word 'imagine' loosely; his 'I imagine' equals 'I suppose'. Guildenstern, worried by their descent into a world in which the law of probability no longer operates, accuses him of a more serious lack of imagination.

I'm afraid—: Once again Rosencrantz uses an expression in a common, casual, not very intense way. Guildenstern takes it more seriously and admits that he is afraid

redistribution of wealth: because Guildenstern has had to hand over money eighty-nine times

essence of a man . . . unremembered past: deep down, unknown to himself, Guildenstern is willing his own losses as a punishment for sins that he can longer remember having committed

children of Israel: whom God, as related in the Bible, in Exodus, led safely out of Egypt, through the desert, and into the Promised Land

Lot's wife: who, in fleeing from the cities of Sodom and Gomorrah, which God was destroying, looked back and was, as a punishment, turned into a pillar of salt (see the Bible, Genesis 19:26)

syllogism: a logical structure in which two propositions, known as premisses, lead to a conclusion. Thus, if all men are mortal (first, or major, premiss), and if Socrates is a man (second, or minor, premiss), we may safely conclude that Socrates is mortal

One, he had never known anything like it: reference to the 1967 edition suggests that 'had' is a misprint for 'has'. The 1967 reading preserves the sequence of tenses better

the first thing you remember: Guildenstern is asking about Rosencrantz's earliest memories. Rosencrantz misinterprets him as asking about those memories which first enter his head in response to the question. Rosencratnz then says, nonsensically, that he has forgotten the first thing which he remembers

I've forgotten the question: in the 1967 edition this exchange continued: 'GUIL: 'How long have you suffered from a bad memory?' ROS: 'I can't remember'

Act 1 (pages 12–16)

Rosencrantz and Guildenstern have been 'sent for' by the king, though they do not know for what purpose. The sound of distant music is heard, and a small troupe of wandering actors appears.

NOTES AND GLOSSARY:

We were sent for: the first reference to Shakespeare's text, where (II. 2) Claudius greets Rosencrantz and Guildenstern with the words: 'The need we have to use you did provoke/Our hasty sending'

Syllogism the second: Guildenstern's syllogism is valid provided that we interpret his initial premiss as meaning that 'probability is a factor which *always* operates within natural forces whether or not it operates elsewhere' (that is, from its non-operation a conclusion follows, though none follows from its operation)

the probability of the *first* part: Guildenstern is asking Rosencrantz to assume that probably the laws of probability do not apply 'within un-, sub- or supernatural forces'. But in saying that *probably* they do not apply the assumption is being made that they do. However, if they *do* apply 'within un-, sub- or supernatural forces' then Rosencrantz and Guildenstern are not under the influence of such forces since they now live in a world in which the laws of probability no longer apply. Much of the humour of the passage, which is more evident in performance than in detailed reading, comes from Rosencrantz's being quite unable to follow Guildenstern's contorted arguments

the fortuitous and the ordained: the individual coin is 'free' to fall on either its head or its tail; which way it falls is a matter of chance (is 'fortuitous'). But over an extended run coins will fall as often one way as the other, and this equitableness is 'ordained'. At this point there exist clear parallels between *Rosencrantz and Guildenstern* and Stoppard's only, and very nearly contemporary, novel *Lord Malquist and Mr Moon* (1966). Whether things happen by chance or because they are part of a grand but as yet undiscovered design is a question which obsesses Moon, the novel's hero, who wants to know if 'there is something going on besides a lot of accidents'. He plans (p. 139) to produce a wall-chart (a 'diagram of everything that counts') which will enable him 'to discover the grand design, find out if there is one, or if it's all random – if there's anything to it'. Both Moon and Rosencrantz and Guildenstern run up against the fact, which they never wholly recognise, of their being characters in someone else's fiction, condemned to make their way through a script over which they have no control and to discuss their freedom or lack of freedom in words which they did not choose and which they are not free to reject

the wind of a windless day: Stoppard is fond of reminding us that his characters are actors upon a stage. This stage is fixed within an enclosed building in which there is no wind, but which represents an outdoor location where the wind freely blows

the toenails on the other hand: the joke, which did not figure in the 1967 text, depends upon taking a colloquial expression literally. In *The Real Inspector Hound* the inspector's request that Lady Muldoon put herself completely in his hands is similarly misinterpreted ('Don't, Inspector', she replies, 'I love Albert') leaving the inspector to protest stiffly that she has not grasped his meaning. Jokes of this type have long been steady favourites in English comedy. In W. S. Gilbert's* *Foggerty's Fairy* (1889) there occurs the following very Stoppard-like piece of dialogue: 'TALBOT: Then there's the breakfast, and the carriages, and a new pair of trousers bought expressly for the occasion! MISS SPIFF: Don't distress yourself, I'll take them off your hands. TALBOT: They're not on my hands –'.

But then he called our names: these words are significant in terms of the overall development of the play; see below, p. 33, the note on the play's final stage-direction. 'That man, a foreigner, he woke us up' is Stoppard's sly allusion to himself

We better get on: (*colloquial*) we had better start moving. In the 1967 edition, in response to Rosencrantz's 'You might

*William Schwenck Gilbert (1836–1911), a prolific dramatist, is now principally remembered as the librettist of the Savoy operas, for which Arthur Seymour Sullivan (1842–1900) provided the music. Gilbert's Shakespearean burlesque *Rosencrantz and Guildenstern* (first staged 1891) is a possible influence upon Stoppard, and is discussed in Part 3 of these Notes.

well think', Guildenstern says: 'Without much conviction; we better get on'. The words also recall 'We're getting on', spoken by Hamm, a character in Samuel Beckett's play *Endgame* (1958). There is a certain appropriateness about having Hamm's words recalled in a play based on *Hamlet* but indebted to Beckett

We are entitled to some direction: another of Stoppard's theatrical jokes. In addition to the obvious meaning this is also a reference to the work of a theatrical director

A man breaking his journey . . . mistaken for a deer: Guildenstern means that an unusual experience, when confined to a single person, can easily be explained away. When the experience is confirmed by a second person, however, the first person accepts it as being both 'real' and unusual. With every subsequent confirmation it becomes less and less unusual. In *Jumpers* (1972), Stoppard's first full-length play after *Rosencrantz and Guildenstern are Dead*, Dotty, the female lead, protests that seeing photographs of men walking about on the moon would be like seeing a unicorn on the television news-programmes. Neither the moon nor unicorns can have their former emotional impact after they have been made common by television or the press

---

Act 1 (pages 16–25)

The players, anxious to make money in hard times, offer the full use of the members of their company to Rosencrantz and Guildenstern. Eventually, after repeated misunderstandings, the offer is declined.

NOTES AND GLOSSARY:

we grow rusty: 'Do they grow rusty?', Hamlet asks Rosencrantz (*Hamlet* II.2.335) who, in Shakespeare's play, assures him that they do not

We can give you a tumble: the first of the Player's long series of sexual innuendoes

pirated from the Italian: Italian *novellas* (short novels) were a rich source of material for Elizabethan dramatists. *The Murder of Gonzago*, the play with which Hamlet tests Claudius's guilt, is, he assures Claudius, based upon a story that is 'extant, and writ in very choice Italian' (*Hamlet* III.2.256)

***his* name's Guildenstern, and *I'm* Rosencrantz:** in *Hamlet* II.2.33–4 Claudius says: 'Thanks, Rosencrantz and gentle Guildenstern.' Gertrude adds: 'Thanks, Guildenstern and gentle Rosencrantz.' The changing of the order of the names is most probably an example of the Elizabethans' love of formal patterning in language or is perhaps Gertrude's way of registering that neither Rosencrantz nor Guildenstern has priority over the other. It has, however, been interpreted by some directors as evidence that Claudius addresses each by the other's name. It is this interpretation which Stoppard chooses here and elsewhere (especially pp. 27–8) to develop

I recognized you at once—: either Rosencrantz interrupts the Player before he has had time to finish his compliment, or the Player quickly adds 'as fellow artists' when Rosencrantz challenges him to make good his flattery. In either case the humour depends upon the fact that most sentences begin in ways which allow more than one conclusion to be reached

performance . . . patronage: the Player is saying that the work of art (the play) requires someone to perform it, and someone to pay the performers. Both the players and those who pay them ('gentlemen') are thus 'fellow artists'

Don't clap . . . old world: 'Don't clap too hard – it's a very old building' are words spoken to an unenthusiastic audience by Archie Rice, as a part of his comic routine, in *The Entertainer* (1957), a play by John Osborne (*b.* 1929). There is also a recollection of Miranda's speech in Shakespeare's *The Tempest* (1611): 'O' wonder!/How many goodly creatures are there here!/How beauteous mankind is! O brave new world,/That has such people in't!' (V.I.182)

transvestite melodrama: women were not allowed to appear upon the Elizabethan stage. Young boys, dressed in women's clothes, impersonated them

Getting warm, am I?: (a) 'Am I describing what you wish to see performed?' and (b) 'Am I becoming sexually titillating?'

A nest of children: in *Hamlet* II.2.336 Rosencrantz tells Hamlet that the travelling players have lost popularity to 'an eyrie of children, little eyases, that cry out . . . these are now the fashion' ('eyrie' = nest; 'eyases' = young hawks). Shakespeare is alluding to a company of young actors established at the Blackfriars' (indoor or 'private') theatre in London in 1600

There's one born: alluding to the proverbial saying: 'There's a fool born every minute'

stoop . . . bent: words which indicate that the Player is offering Rosencrantz the sexual use of his company. 'Bent' is slang for 'homosexual'

I have influence yet: 'yet' means 'still'. The player takes it to mean 'but' and thinks it begins a new clause; hence his question. A similar joke occurs in *The Real Inspector Hound* where one character says, 'It's wonderful how you country people really know weather', only to receive the reply: 'Know whether what?'

Rape of the Sabine Women: Romulus, legendary founder of Rome, peopled his city by detaining in it by force the wives and daughters of the neighbouring Sabine tribe. This enforced detention became a popular subject in pictorial art, but what the Player is offering Guildenstern is clearly a very seedy presentation of the same. In view of the bawdy double-meanings that here abound 'uncut' is probably meant to suggest that Alfred is uncircumcised

taking either part: adopting either the active or the passive role in homosexual love-making

It could have been . . . . rabble of prostitutes: Guildenstern believes that it is fate, not chance, which is controlling their lives. He is looking for a portent, for some occurrence that will indicate to him what he is supposed to do. Of the fated and significant encounters that he had imagined this meeting with the sordid players is the least dignified, the least suggestive of a high course for him carved out by his controlling fate

trade: a cant term for (paid) homosexual activity

every exit being an entrance somewhere else: partly a sly allusion to the structure of Stoppard's play, and also the grossest of his play's homosexual innuendoes

***The* PLAYER *spits . . . from where he stands*:** in the 1967 edition the Player's disdain had been made vocal. After spitting at the coin he says: 'Leave it lying there. Perhaps when we come back this way we'll be that much cheaper'

we could create a dramatic precedent here: once again Stoppard plays around with his audience's awareness of itself as an audience and of the play as play (Guildenstern is directed to look 'at the audience'). Guildenstern says that Alfred and he could commit an indecency never before seen upon the English stage, and could thus regard themselves as innovators

Matri, patri . . .: matricide, patricide (or parricide) . . ., the killing of a mother, father, brother, sister, and wife

vice versa: gods aspiring to maidenheads. There is also a pun on 'vice'

we'll let you know: the established phrase used in casting sessions as a tactful indication that the applicant has been unsuccessful. Guildenstern thus indicates, using appropriate theatre language, that he does not require Alfred's services

Act 1 (pages 26–39)

As the players are about to perform their play they are interrupted by the first of the extended extracts from *Hamlet*. Claudius, after displaying uncertainty as to which of them is which, sets Rosencrantz and Guildenstern the task of finding the cause of Hamlet's increasingly strange behaviour. Once left alone the two plan how they are to proceed (without ever proceeding). To help them in their task they play a trial game of questions and answers, but manage only to confuse themselves further. Hamlet enters and, as Act 1 ends, they are about to try out their non-existent skills on him.

NOTES AND GLOSSARY:

OPHELIA *runs on . . . followed by* HAMLET: the 1967 text added the following: 'Note: The resemblance between HAMLET and the PLAYER is superficial but noticeable'

OPHELIA *has been sewing*: this stage-direction closely paraphrases Ophelia's speech (*Hamlet* II.1). The rest of this section should be compared with *Hamlet* II.2

We'll soon be home and high: this, and the nonsense which follows, is intended to indicate that Rosencrantz and Guildenstern are nearing hysteria. Rosencrantz, in particular, is upset by Claudius's inability to remember his name

why don't you make up your mind: Rosencrantz is prepared to be known as either Rosencrantz or Guildenstern, provided that he is thereafter known consistently by whichever name is chosen

Nor did we come all this way for a christening: a half-reference to 'The Journey of the Magi' (1927) by T. S. Eliot (1888–1965): 'were we led all that way for/Birth or

Death? There was a Birth, certainly,/We had evidence and no doubt. I had seen birth and death,/But had thought they were different'. (The Magi were the wise men who visited the Christ-child in the stable at Bethlehem. Christening, or baptism, is the first and greatest of the Christian initiation ceremonies, at which – though it is not an essential part of the service – candidates are formally given Christian names.) That Stoppard has Eliot's poem in mind is made clearer a few lines further on when Guildenstern mentions both birth and death.

There is also a possible allusion to *The Importance of Being Earnest* (first performed in 1895) by Oscar Wilde (1854–1900) in which much of the comedy involves changes of characters' names and in which the two male leads independently arrange to be christened Ernest. There are extended allusions to Wilde's play in *Travesties.*

At least we are presented with alternatives: each knows that he is *either* Rosencrantz *or* Guildenstern

Give us this day our daily mask: a reference to one of the petitions of the Our Father ('Give us this day our daily bread'), the prayer taught by Christ to his disciples (see the Bible, Matthew 6 and Luke 11). The theme of disguise is prominent in *Hamlet*

***a dying fall*:** another Shakespeare allusion: 'That strain again! it had a dying fall' (*Twelfth Night* I.1.4). Compare also T. S. Eliot's 'The Love Song of J. Alfred Prufrock' (1917): 'I know the voices dying with a dying fall/Beneath the music from a farther room'

Elephantine: like an elephant, an animal that traditionally never forgets. It is not in the length of Claudius's memory but in what it will prompt him to do that Rosencrantz is interested

a royal retainer: a royal retainer is (a) a paid servant to a king, or (b) the fee paid to such a servant in order to secure his services

A short, blunt human pyramid: in *Jumpers* Stoppard makes his actor-acrobats construct a human pyramid

I feel like a spectator: Stoppard's playing around with our usual notion of theatre (so that, for instance, a theatre becomes a building into which audiences go to be watched by actors) is taken much further in *The Real Inspector Hound*, in which we watch two people watching a play. They are seated on the opposite side of the stage from us, as though we were backstage

We could play at questions: play a game in which the players are allowed to ask each other only questions, and in which they are penalised for statements, exclamations, repetitions, etc. *Rosencrantz and Guildenstern* is a play about playing; about actors playing parts, and people playing games, and about people who are the playthings of forces which they do not understand

One–love: one, nil. The scoring system is loosely based upon that used in lawn tennis

Whose serve?: 'to serve' is to propel the ball into your opponent's part of the court at the start of each unit of play in tennis, table-tennis, and related games

Game point: Guildenstern means that whoever scores the next point wins the game

***non sequiturs*:** (*Latin*, it does not follow) a stage in an argument, or the conclusion to one, that is not deducible from the preceding stage or stages is known as a *non sequitur*

Match point to me: the match consists of three games, each containing three points. The first player to reach three points wins the game; the first to reach two games wins the match

How should I begin?: J. Alfred Prufrock, in T. S. Eliot's 'The Love Song of J. Alfred Prufrock' asks: 'And should I then presume?/And how should I begin?'. Eliot's poem contains many allusions to *Hamlet*

Statement: failing to understand the play-acting which Guildenstern is suggesting that they undertake, Rosencrantz reverts to the game that they were playing earlier

He slipped in: Shakespeare's Hamlet accuses Claudius of having 'popp'd in between th'election and my hopes' (V.2.65), by which he means that Claudius has ascended the Danish throne in defiance of approved constitutional procedures and has thus deprived Hamlet of a position that rightfully belongs to him. Stoppard's Rosencrantz interprets 'slipped in' bawdily

Would you go so far?: Rosencrantz asks: 'Would you go so far as to suggest that your mother is guilty of incest and adultery?' Guildenstern, in the character of Hamlet, assumes that the question is: 'Would you go so far as to commit incest and adultery?'

Good lads, how do you both?: once again *Hamlet* II.2 should be consulted. In the 1967 text Stoppard indicated that the scene should end 'overtaken by rising music and fading light'

Act 2 (pages 40–45)

The attempt to discover the secret of Hamlet's melancholy has proved unsuccessful.

NOTES AND GLOSSARY:

S'blood: an oath; an abbreviated form of 'By Christ's blood'

***flourish*:** fanfare

Gentlemen: that is, Rosencrantz and Guildenstern. Hamlet tells them that they are welcome and then offers to shake hands with them

The appurtenance .... than yours: Hamlet says that there are actions ('fashion and ceremony') appointed by good manners to accompany a spoken welcome. He observes these customary actions, by shaking hands with Rosencrantz and Guildenstern, so as to assure them that they are not less welcome than the players, whom he intends to greet enthusiastically

in this garb: in this manner

hawk from a handsaw: perhaps Hamlet is claiming he can distinguish between two birds (handsaw = hernshaw, or heron) or between two tradesmen's tools (hawk = a square board used by plasterers) or perhaps his words are to be taken as they stand as a mark of his feigned madness. Stoppard's Rosencrantz and Guildenstern have no clearer understanding of Hamlet's precise meaning than have modern commentators

swaddling clouts: clothes in which babies were tightly wrapped

Roscius: Quintus Roscius Gallus (*d.*62 BC) was the most famous comic actor in ancient Rome

close to the chest: an image from card-play. By holding his cards close to his chest a player lessens the chances of their being overseen

all down the line: once again the imagery is taken from tennis, in which a ball struck into the opponent's court so as to land as close as possible to the boundary line is likely to prove a winning shot

on the wrong foot: in tennis parlance, to catch one's opponent on the wrong foot is to have him prepared to move in the wrong direction and unprepared in consequence to move to where the ball lands. Tennis (though not in its modern form) was a well-liked game among Elizabethan courtiers, but it is its highly formalised character, dependent on rules and conventions, that appeals to Stoppard

He murdered us: a humorous exaggeration of a kind much used in modern sports reporting, but ironical in view of what the audience knows is going to happen

Pragmatism: reliance upon experience and practical possibility rather than upon principles worked out in advance of, and used in order to decide upon, action

***He studies the floor*:** this stage-direction is more strictly such than most, since it directs the audience's attention to the stage. Taken together with the earlier reference to the draught it serves to emphasise that though Rosencrantz and Guildenstern's position is unlocalised ('You seem to have no conception of where we stand') they are all the time on the stage of a public theatre

a shambles: a mess; originally a place where animals were butchered

Act 2 (pages 45–53)

Hamlet orders the players to prepare a performance of 'The Murder of Gonzago' into which a speech of his own composing will be inserted. Rosencrantz and Guildenstern renew their acquaintance with the players, who are hurt and vengeful after their last encounter.

NOTES AND GLOSSARY:

Follow that lord: that is, Polonius

So you've caught up: Guildenstern means that the Player has at last reached the court. (By contrast, such is the nature of Stoppard's stage illusion, Rosencrantz and Guildenstern have reached it without having had to travel.) The Player's cold reply seems to indicate that he interprets Guildenstern's words as meaning: 'So you've got even with us (for not attending to your previous performance)'

every gesture, every pose: the reading 'every prose', found in some copies, is a misprint

peeped through his fingers: in the players' 'transvestite melodrama' (p. 17) Rosalinda is represented by a male actor: hence 'peeped through *his* fingers'

obscene: that is 'obscene' which takes place off-stage. The term derives from the ancient Greek theatre in which most action was merely reported as having happened elsewhere

with a vengeance: as a figure of speech this means, roughly, 'and no mistake!'. Guildenstern's remark that it is an idiomatic expression, not one to be taken literally, confirms the interpretation of 'So you've caught up' given above

Classical: the Player means, ostensibly, that Hamlet likes serious, established drama. Rosencrantz, carrying on the camp badinage which characterised his earlier conversations with the Player, assumes him to mean that Hamlet shares the sexual preferences of the peoples of the ancient (Classical) world. Presumably he has the Greeks in mind

losing your heads: (a) making fools of yourselves, and (b) being executed

We don't know how to *act*: one of the points in the play in which a word ('act') has reference both to the world of the theatre and to the world outside the theatre

nothing .... honoured: Anderson, the Professor of Ethics in *Professional Foul* (1977) – a much more obviously serious play than *Rosencrantz and Guildenstern are Dead* – holds to a point of view markedly similar to that put forward by the Player. Human rights, Anderson argues, are fictions which we are obliged to treat as if they were truths

he's in love with *his* daughter: Stoppard is here revelling in the notorious difficulties to which a careless use of pronouns can plunge the English speaker. The Player means that Polonius thinks that Hamlet is in love with Polonius's daughter. Rosencrantz thinks that he means that Hamlet is in love with Hamlet's daughter. He then misinterprets Guildenstern's explanation, and so supposes that Polonius is in love with Ophelia

a show-stopper: another verbal tease. A 'show-stopper' is a song, or a dance-routine, or a piece of comic business that is so successful that the performance is halted to allow for applause. But it is not only success that stops shows. *Jumpers*, Stoppard's first full-length play after *Rosencrantz and Guildenstern are Dead*, begins with a show-stopping routine of the latter sort

"Hey you, whatsyername! . . . there!": Rosencrantz's words are likely to set up two echoes in an audience's mind: (a) of the messenger, banging upon the shutters and calling out their names, and (b) of Christ's words to the dead Lazarus: 'he cried out with a loud voice, "Lazarus, come out." The dead man came out, his hands and feet bound with bandages, and his face wrapped with a cloth' (see the Bible, John 11: 43–4)

"Saul of Tarsus yet!": all early Christians were Jews. Stoppard mimics conventionally Jewish turns of phrase – 'yet', 'Tarsus-Schmarsus', 'already'. Compare *Lord Malquist and Mr Moon*: '*Jackson-schmackson*, thought Moon who sometimes wanted to be a Jew but had only the most superficial understanding of how to go about it' (p. 28). Saul of Tarsus was known as Paul after his conversion to Christianity (see the Bible, Acts 13: 9)

A Christian, a Moslem and a Jew: this joke follows on from the reference to Saul of Tarsus, one of the most famous of all religious converts. In the joke the Moslem is a Jew who has been converted to Islam. His Jewish questioner calls him by his pre-conversion name. The Moslem then refers to his friend, formerly a Moslem but now a convert to Christianity, by *his* pre-conversion name. A similar, and similarly lame, joke occurs in *Lord Malquist and Mr Moon*: ' "What's your name, O'Hara, your Christian name?" / "Abendigo." / "You're a convert?" / "My whole life I am a convert." ' (p. 50)

Act 2 (pages 54–9)

Claudius is informed of the players' arrival and of Hamlet's interest in their work. He plots to eavesdrop on his nephew's conversations with Ophelia. While the players are rehearsing their play we hear of the result of Claudius's spying and of his determination to send Hamlet to England.

NOTES AND GLOSSARY:

o'erraught: overtook

closely: privately (that is, without making any public fuss)

Affront: meet (compare 'confront') – not 'offend' or 'assault'

Why can't *we* go by *them*?: another reference to the conventions of the stage. The acting area does not move, nor do Rosencrantz and Guildenstern ever leave it. We agree to accept that this fixed area represents first one place, then another. If we did not do so and supposed instead, as some classical theorists have insisted that we should, that the stage represents the same piece of countryside or court throughout the play, the effect would be one of everybody's coming to visit Rosencrantz and Guildenstern and of an unnatural concentration of activity within one small area

***making his quietus*:** the reference is to Hamlet's most famous soliloquy ('To be, or not to be') in which he contemplates suicide (*Hamlet* III.1.56ff. especially l. 75)

No point in looking . . . whites of his eyes: a confusion of two sayings: (a) 'Never look a gift horse in the mouth' and (b) 'Don't shoot until you see the whites of his eyes'. The first saying instructs the recipient of a gift not to question its value: it would be proper to assess (by inspecting its teeth) the age of a horse which you were thinking of buying but improper to do so if the horse were a gift. The second saying means 'Save your ammunitition until you are sure of your target', but can also be used metaphorically

orisons: prayers

***The* PLAYER *lifts . . . leaps away*:** Rosencrantz assumes that once again the player is standing on his dropped coin

I put my foot down: in part a literal description of what the player has done, but also a colloquial phrase meaning 'I asserted my authority'

When Queens . . . passed down in the blood: a more forthright version of the same joke appears in *Lord Malquist and Mr Moon*, p. 67: 'the Malquists in common with other families of equal style and breeding excrete and procreate by a cerebral process the secret of which is passed down in the blood'

avuncular: having the (pleasant) characteristics of an uncle

Act 2 (pages 59–72)

The players continue their rehearsal, watched by Rosencrantz and Guildenstern who do not understand that their own deaths are being shown to them. Claudius enters and sends Rosencrantz and Guildenstern in search of Hamlet, who has murdered Polonius. After yet another inconclusive meeting with Hamlet they learn that they are to accompany him to England.

NOTES AND GLOSSARY:

You're not getting across!: if the players were 'getting across' (making their point) Guildenstern would know what he was supposed to think

chaos on the night: a comic reversal of the theatrical slogan: 'It'll be all right on the night'

"just desserts" and "tragic irony"; the players specialise in death scenes. There are plenty of these, including scenes in which the wicked get their just deserts ('desserts' is a misprint) and scenes in which the innocent die as a result of cruel ironies of circumstance

The bad end unhappily . . . . what tragedy means: in the Irish playwright Oscar Wilde's (1854–1900) *The Importance of Being Earnest* (1895) Miss Prism describes her only novel as one in which 'the good ended happily, and the bad unhappily. That is what fiction means'

a beginning, middle and end: according to the Greek philosopher and literary critic Aristotle (384–322BC) 'a tragedy is an imitation of an action that is complete in itself . . . which has beginning, middle, and end' (*De Poetica*, Chapter VII). Birdboot, the drama critic in Stoppard's *The Real Inspector Hound*, says of the play that he is reviewing that 'it has a beginning, a middle and I have no doubt it will prove to have an end'

I'd prefer art to mirror life: compare Hamlet's speech to the players: 'O'erstep not the modesty of nature; for anything so overdone is from the purpose of playing, whose end, both at the first and now, was and is, to hold, as 'twere, the mirror up to nature' (*Hamlet* III.2.20ff.)

Lucianus: Lucianus is the name of the character in *The Murder of Gonzago* whose murder of his uncle conveys to Claudius Hamlet's desire to threaten him

arras: a tapestry wall-hanging, used as decoration and also to exclude draughts

***oedipal embrace*:** Oedipus, king of Thebes, was, according to ancient legend, separated from his parents as a young child. When he grew up, without being aware of who they were he killed his father and married his mother. The 'Oedipus complex' is the name given by the Viennese psychoanalyst Sigmund Freud (1856–1939) to the unconscious male desire to repeat the crimes of Oedipus. One of Freud's disciples, Ernest Jones (1879–1958), was of the opinion that

Shakespeare's Hamlet evidenced the complex, and thus both hated and envied Claudius (who had done what he had himself secretly wished to do)

hoist by their own petard: blown up by their own bomb. Hamlet uses the phrase (III.4.202ff.) to refer to his intention to destroy Rosencrantz and Guildenstern by altering the letter which they are carrying to the English king

A slaughterhouse: a word that recalls 'shambles' (p. 44)

eight corpses: as is pointed out in the final note in the present section (see p. 33) the 1967 version of the play has a different ending. In that version the two ambassadors list the names of the eight people who have been killed, thus recalling this line

the whisper in their skulls: Stoppard here recalls the opening lines of T. S. Eliot's 'Whispers of Immortality': 'Webster was much possessed by death/And saw the skull beneath the skin'. John Webster (?1580–?1625) was a dramatist noted for his scenes of death, sensuality, and violence

a sheep – or a lamb: a reference to the proverb: 'as well be hanged for a sheep as a lamb' (meaning that, where penalties do not discriminate between a greater and a lesser offence, one might as well be guilty of the greater)

to suspend one's disbelief: the English poet and critic Samuel Taylor Coleridge (1772–1834) wrote, in *Biographia Literaria* (1817), of 'that willing suspension of disbelief for the moment, which constitutes poetic faith'. His words, when applied to the drama, suggest that spectators are willing, while a performance lasts, to suspend (but not to dispense with) their knowledge that what is taking place on stage is an acted representation of reality rather than reality itself. Stoppard's Player complains that, when his actor really died, the spectators thought that he was merely acting

Friends both . . . . haste in this: this speech (compare *Hamlet*. IV.1.32–7) in which Claudius gives Rosencrantz and Guildenstern a genuine task to do was added by Stoppard at the request of Laurence Olivier, director of the National Theatre

ROS'S ***trousers slide slowly down*:** Stoppard, with characteristic diffidence, has described *Rosencrantz and Guildenstern are Dead* as being 'slightly literate music-hall perhaps' (Hayman, *Tom Stoppard* (1978), p. 5). The vaudeville element in this comic routine is obvious: the literary element is derived from Samuel Beckett. At the end of *Waiting for Godot*, Vladimir and Estragon try to work out how they may best hang themselves. Estragon removes the rope which serves him as a belt, and his trousers fall down. Thus the end of the play reveals man's own latter end. Stoppard refers to Beckett by name ('Wham, bam, thank you Sam') at the close of *Jumpers*. He also refers to 'the clown's indignity of fallen trousers' in *Lord Malquist and Mr Moon* (p. 145)

they've done with us: 'they've done with us' = 'they have finished with us', but is misinterpreted by Guildenstern who asks: 'What have they done with us?'

Act 3 (pages 73–96)

It is dark. Rosencrantz and Guildenstern, aboard ship bound for England, open Claudius's letter to the English king and discover from it that Hamlet is to be killed. When they fall asleep Hamlet replaces Claudius's letter with one of his own, sentencing its bearers to death. Next morning Rosencrantz and Guildenstern find that the players, fearing the displeasure of Claudius, have stowed away. Pirates attack. Everybody hides, and Hamlet, under cover of confusion, makes his escape, leaving Rosencrantz and Guildenstern once again unsure of how to proceed. The audience, however, knows that ahead of them lies England and death. The play ends with the reports of the ambassadors from England, delivered as the stage slowly darkens.

NOTES AND GLOSSARY:

Are you there? . . . . Well, that's cleared that up: the mistakes that are made when one is unable to see are humorously (and appropriately) exploited in Stoppard's radio play *Artist Descending a Staircase* (broadcast in 1972) in which it is the radio audience which is kept in the dark

In out here?: 'somebody might come in' suggests the stage of an enclosed theatre (where the actors who play Rosencrantz and Guildenstern really are); 'out here' suggests the open air and the open sea (where Rosencrantz and Guildenstern are supposed to be). 'In out here?' combines both suggestions

Nice bit of planking: Rosencrantz draws attention to the wooden stage which represents the ship's deck

game of tag: a children's game in which one child tries to touch others who run away from him. Once a child has been touched (or tagged) it is his turn to act as pursuer

Other side, I think: Guildenstern wants Rosencrantz to vomit over the side of the boat that is not into the wind. Later (p. 88) Hamlet spits into the wind, with predictable results

in peril on the sea: words taken from the refrain to the hymn 'Eternal Father, strong to save' by William Whiting (1825–78)

cue: words or actions which indicate to an actor that it is his turn to enter onstage or to begin speaking

Will *he* be there?: Rosencrantz thinks that the king mentioned by Guildenstern is Claudius. Guildenstern corrects him

we're finished: dramatic irony. The audience knows that Rosencrantz and Guildenstern are to be killed

You've got it: Guildenstern means: 'You have understood the situation'. Rosencrantz once again misunderstands: hence the confusion which follows

cartographers: map-makers

clutching at straws: to keep afloat by clutching at a straw is a proverbial illustration of desperate measures taken in extremity. Because sun-baked bricks were made by mixing mud and chopped straw Rosencrantz's mind, which has itself been clutching at straws throughout the play, moves to a still more absurd version of the proverb. The same joke appears in *Lord Malquist and Mr Moon* (p. 52) where Moon thinks: 'I clutch at straws but what good's a brick to a drowning man?'

As Socrates ... put it: Socrates (469–399BC), an ancient Greek teacher and philosopher, was sentenced to death for, allegedly, corrupting the intellects, and hence the morals, of the young. In the time before his sentence was carried out he meditated much upon his own impending death and upon death in general, though he seems never to have reached the conclusion which Guildenstern ascribes to him. In his *Apology*, written by his disciple Plato (*c*.427–348BC), Socrates argues that 'we shall see that there is great reason to hope that death is good ... either death is a state of nothingness and utter unconsciousness, or ... there is a change and migration of the soul from this world to another'

ventages: stops: Guildenstern is quoting Hamlet's speech (*Hamlet* III.2.350ff.)

All in the same boat: this colloquial expression which is literally true here is a typical Stoppard witticism

Are we all right for England?: Rosencrantz means: 'Are we on the right course for England?' The Player interprets him as meaning: 'Are we going to be acceptable in England?'

a second husband: the Player's allusion is to words spoken in *Hamlet* (but not recorded in Stoppard's play) by the player-queen: 'In second husband let me be accurst;/None wed the second but who kill'd the first . . . . A second time I kill my husband dead,/When second husband kisses me in bed' (III.2.174ff.)

We can do what we like: Shakespeare, into whose play Rosencrantz and Guildenstern are so firmly locked, has no scene set on board the ship carrying Hamlet to England. Thus, if we grant Stoppard's basic conceit, we may suppose that Rosencrantz and Guildenstern are indeed free to do and to say what they will, unconstrained by the need to follow details of Shakespeare's play. Of course they are also, but without their knowing, locked with equal firmness into Stoppard's text

delusions of imprisonment: compare: 'Denmark's a prison' (*Hamlet* II.2.244)

camels, chameleons: compare *Hamlet* III.2.370ff.

amnesia: loss of memory

paranoia: an obsessive fear that one is being plotted against or otherwise persecuted

myopia: short-sightedness

at his age: hints thrown out by Shakespeare suggest that Hamlet is thirty years old

talking to himself: one of the few places in which W. S. Gilbert's *Rosencrantz and Guildenstern* (see footnote above, p. 16, and see also Part 3 of the present Notes) may have influenced a detail in Stoppard's text. In Gilbert's burlesque it is Hamlet's habit of soliloquising that especially distresses Gertrude

***the* PIRATES *attack*:** compare *Hamlet* IV.6.10ff.

***not a pick up*:** Stoppard's direction indicates that Rosencrantz's 'Dead?' is not an attempt at supplying the word that the Player is after. Rosencrantz merely wants to ask whether Hamlet is dead

Not from his mouth . . . truly deliver: in the 1967 edition this speech is printed, following the received text of *Hamlet*, as blank verse

Polack: Polish

***overtaken by dark and music*:** the original ending, as represented by the 1967 text, is different; it was altered during rehearsals at the National Theatre. Instead of the stage being darkened Stoppard followed Shakespeare's text through to its conclusion. Then he added the following scene. The two ambassadors remain, alone, on stage, counting the corpses mentally, and naming them (Claudius, Gertrude, Hamlet, Laertes, Rosencrantz, Guildenstern, Polonius and Ophelia). Offstage there is a sound, and a voice calls out, indistinctly, two names. In response to this summons, deliberately reminiscent of that which aroused Rosencrantz and Guildenstern, the ambassadors leave to find out what is going on. The music that we associate with the players is faintly heard, the house lights come up, and the play ends with an empty, fully lit stage.

Part 3

Commentary

THERE ARE FOUR WAYS of getting to know a play well: by seeing it in performance; by discussing it with friends (and, sometimes better still, with those who are not your friends); by judging it in the light of other, related, plays; and by means of a close line-by-line inspection of its text. Neither performance nor the sort of discussion here envisaged is possible in print. What follows is comparison and analysis.

Travestying Shakespeare

Shakespeare's plays, performed straight or in versions adapted to meet a director's vision of them, dominate the modern stage, are the backbone of commercial, subsidised, and experimental theatre alike, and have an honoured place in television, on the radio, and in the cinema.

The many ways in which Shakespeare is brought to the attention of modern audiences are bewildering. There are Shakespearean ballets and contemporary-dance versions; Shakespearean operas and musicals; productions in all the major languages, including some which 'translate' his words into modern English; productions in mime (for everyone) and in sign-language (for those who cannot hear); productions using puppets. His plays are performed by vast companies in theatres which are relics of the Victorian and Edwardian periods, and by scratch companies on makeshift platforms in schoolrooms, prisons, or outside in the rain. Some productions are surpassingly dull, others fill the stage with character, and action, and colour, but all testify to the central place which Shakespeare holds upon the Western stage.

This unquestioning acceptance of Shakespeare's immense worth, so that any attempt upon his work, however routine or ill-conceived, is assumed to be safe box-office, is not something about which those really interested in the theatre can be entirely happy, for it may simply be evidence of an uncreative aesthetic conservatism (of liking blindly what one has been told is good). But it is a fact, and one which some modern directors and playwrights have exploited in order to bring into prominence their own political or social points of view. Edward Bond's *Bingo: Scenes of Money and Death* (1974) deliberately sought to anger playgoers by its portrayal of a Shakespeare who glimpses in his plays a freer, better order of living, but who in his dealings with the people around him suppresses these insights and reverts to the cruelties of conduct that were standard and acceptable in his day.* Howard Brenton in *Thirteenth Night*, a title which is itself a Shakespearean allusion, has reworked *Macbeth* almost but not quite beyond recognition until it becomes a commentary on the state of politics, and in particular on the future of socialism, in twentieth-century Britain.†

Such explicitly political revamping of Shakespeare is likely to be modern, but it is wrong to suppose that thoroughgoing adaptations of his work are exclusively of recent origin. One special sort, the 'burlesque' or affectionate parody, was especially popular in the Victorian period when it helped to counter without in any way destroying the otherwise excessive veneration in which Shakespeare's name was held.‡ (Nor was Shakespeare alone in being treated in this way; Queen Victoria herself was the subject of humorous, and not always affectionate, music hall songs.) Such burlesques assume as a matter of course that Shakespeare's text is at least moderately well known. Because of its immense fame *Hamlet* attracted a larger than usual number of comic adaptations, many of which are listed, after serious editions of the play, in the catalogue of the British Library under the heading 'Travesties' (itself, surely not by coincidence, the title of one of Stoppard's later plays).

A Victorian burlesque *Hamlet*

The first of the travesties listed in the British Library catalogue, though a very late example of *Hamlet* burlesque, is W. S. Gilbert's *Rosencrantz and Guildenstern*, the only burlesque version of *Hamlet* with which Stoppard is likely to have been acquainted.** There is not much, however, that suggests any great spread or depth of influence. Gilbert's piece is relentlessly trivial and its distortion of Shakespeare's plot is extreme: Stoppard, by way of contrast, leaves Shakespeare's plot intact. From Gilbert's version the intense emotional pressures that prompt Hamlet both to take action and to delay taking action are missing

*Edward Bond (*b.*1934) is also the author of *Lear* (1972), one of the most ambitious dramatic reworkings of a Shakespeare play yet undertaken.

†Howard Brenton (*b.*1942). His other plays include *The Churchill Play* (1974), *Epsom Downs* (1977), and *The Romans in Britain* (1980).

‡These burlesques, including Gilbert's *Rosencrantz and Guildenstern*, are best read in *Nineteenth Century Shakespeare Burlesques*, introduced by Stanley Wells, 5 volumes, Diploma Press, London, 1977. These volumes reprint thirty-three burlesques, ten of which are travesties of *Hamlet*.

***Rosencrantz and Guildenstern* first appeared in print in 1874 but was not staged until 1891. The most convenient modern text for those who cannot consult the 5-volume *Nineteenth Century Shakespeare Burlesques* is in *Plays by W. S. Gilbert*, ed. by George Rowell, Cambridge University Press, Cambridge, 1982.

entirely; his dark family troubles are swept humorously away. Claudius is Hamlet's father, Gertrude's husband, nobody's murderer, and the undisputed king of Denmark. His only fault is that he is a dramatist, and Hamlet's strangeness consists of an irritating habit of talking to himself at great length and with undue formality. Gertrude, wishing to reduce her son to serviceable prose, calls to her aid his boyhood friends, Rosencrantz and Guildenstern, little realising that the former is Hamlet's rival for the hand of Ophelia, and is plotting his rival's downfall. His plan is to persuade Hamlet to perform a little known and grossly incompetent five-act tragedy, written by Claudius in his youth and so distasteful to him in his maturer years that he has pledged to have whoever revives it executed. The plan works and Hamlet is disgraced. But instead of being executed (the only thing which dies is Claudius's play) he is sent to England where, Ophelia explains to the court, men with his difficulties of temperament are usually held in the highest esteem. Thus, as is appropriate in a light entertainment staged to raise money for a good cause, everything ends happily.

In which respects, if any, has Gilbert influenced Stoppard? Despite its title, Rosencrantz and Guildenstern are not in the forefront of Gilbert's burlesque: the honour still belongs to Hamlet. And yet the title may well have suggested to Stoppard the possibility of moving peripheral characters to the centre of the stage while having *Hamlet's* more prominent characters wheel about them. Here and there, also, Gilbert has a Stoppard-like joke (Claudius ruefully admits that his play was a success only by virtue of its succeeding the play which preceded it) and once or twice there is the odd phrase or incident that may have lodged in Stoppard's mind. But the chief respect in which Gilbert's and Stoppard's pieces are similar, their heavy emphasis upon theatre and theatricality, may well reflect not the influence of the former upon the latter but rather their common origins in Shakespeare's play.

A modern collage *Hamlet*

Gilbert's *Rosencrantz and Guildenstern* is affectionate parody: its being so is one of the things which it has in common with Stoppard's play. There is nothing which anyone would think affectionate about a much more recent Shakespeare travesty, Charles Marowitz's *Hamlet** (1965), a work which by a curious coincidence had, like *Rosencrantz and Guildenstern are Dead*, its origins in Berlin in the middle 1960s (see above, 'A note on the text').

Marowitz's version cuts and shuffles Shakespeare's text, sometimes, for its own ironical purposes, shifting a speech from one character to

**The Marowitz Shakespeare*, Marion Boyers, London, 1978, includes a text of Marowitz's *Hamlet*.

another. (It is Gertrude, not Hamlet, who says of the elder Hamlet in this version: 'He was a man, take him for all in all / I shall not look upon his like again.') But though Marowitz's recension can look to hostile eyes like a random affair of violent transitions indulged in for their own sake, it is really produced according to a plan and in careful support of its adaptor's moral outlook. Indeed there could hardly be a clearer example of a director's reworking Shakespeare's text in order to give prominence to his own points of view.

Marowitz admires Shakespeare's play for its energy and its simple compellingness in the theatre, but hates it ('hate' is not too strong a word) because it seems to him to have made attractive to us a sort of personality which in his opinion is contemptible and dangerous. Hamlet, for Marowitz, is the type of liberal spirit who, when called upon to act decisively in situations which require action rather than delicate moral argument, cannot do so for fear of violating his own moral sensibility. But the price which such a liberal pays for holding himself intact is enormous: he becomes a mere puppet, with no part to play of his own prompting in the affairs of the world.

Such a view of Hamlet's character, though rarely expressed with such force, is not in fact new. Samuel Johnson, in the eighteenth century, declared Hamlet to be throughout the play 'rather an instrument than an agent'; and Samuel Taylor Coleridge, in the early years of the nineteenth century, spoke of a Hamlet who 'finally gives himself up to his destiny, and, *in the infirmity of his nature*, at last hopelessly places himself in the power and mercy of his enemies'.* What is new is the ruthlessness with which Marowitz cuts up Shakespeare's text in order both to compel an audience to share his view and to make clear his own contempt for Hamlet's character. In Marowitz's version the contrasts between Hamlet and Fortinbras and between Hamlet and Laertes (the first contrast barely developed by Shakespeare; the second developed to Hamlet's advantage) both work to Hamlet's deep discredit. At one point the Ghost so despairs of having Hamlet avenge him that he adopts Fortinbras as son in his place. And though, in the everyday sense of the term, Hamlet is unable to act (much of Marowitz's version consists of Hamlet's *imagined* actions), in the theatrical sense of the term all that he can do is act: he is self-consciously the actor, doing in play what he will not do in reality, and not doing even that well, so that his speeches are reduced to an impotent rhetoric which is booed by his fellows on stage at the same time as they applaud Laertes's forceful speech and action.

*Samuel Johnson (1709–84), poet, critic, lexicographer, and editor of Shakespeare's works. By *agent* Johnson means 'one who acts on his own behalf' (not 'one who acts on behalf of another'). Samuel Taylor Coleridge (1772–1834) was the most eminent poet-critic of the Romantic period.

Clearly as a balanced view of Shakespeare's play Marowitz's version will not do at all: to push an audience's sympathies away from the conscience-stricken Hamlet towards the hyperactive Laertes is to miss the fact that Laertes too, in his dealings with Claudius, is rather an instrument than an agent and blindly serves purposes which in his anger he fails to divine. But as a professedly unbalanced view of Shakespeare's play, true in some of its details however wildly exaggerated its emphases, Marowitz's version will do very well indeed. The brusqueness with which Shakespeare is treated is matched by his adaptor's dismissive treatment of his own audience. Any theatre audience, Marowitz contends, has already settled into a pattern of expectation well before a word is spoken on stage: an audience at a Shakespeare play may have had that pattern set for them years in advance and will have bought their tickets and occupied their seats in the belief that those expectations are to be fulfilled to the letter without in any way being challenged or revised ('Audiences know what to expect', the Player tells Guildenstern, 'and that is all that they are prepared to believe in' – p. 64). Theatre-goers are, Marowitz suggests, as sensitive to what is passing before their eyes as a stopped clock is to the passage of time. The remedy required by both is that they should be given a good shaking to set them ticking again. Shaken, but once again in working order, an audience which has watched the Marowitz *Hamlet* will be more acute and much more wary in its future dealings with Shakespeare's play.

There is no point in accusing Marowitz of arrogance. Of course he is arrogant ('dogmatic' is his word), but that is part of a deliberate policy of annoying his audience. This hostility towards an audience is also not new – there is evidence of it from the Elizabethan period for instance – but its theoretical justification is more recent. Such hostility, however, is hardly to be met with at all in Stoppard's altogether gentler works. Stoppard contents himself with allowing Rosencrantz a protest at the inertness of his audience at that point in the play where, in order to demonstrate the 'misuse of free speech', Rosencrantz shouts 'Fire!'. The audience, naturally, does not respond. Rosencrantz looks out 'with contempt' and, acknowledging the members of the audience directly, tells Guildenstern that 'They should burn to death in their shoes' (p. 44). But the effect of this protest is almost entirely one of amusement. It is worth recalling that Stoppard has become a force in the commercial theatre, something which Marowitz has never been and something which he probably would not wish to be. Clearly, despite the closeness in time of their composition and their common origins in Shakespeare's *Hamlet*, Stoppard's and Marowitz's plays are very different works with little in common.

Stoppard's other *Hamlet*

Recently Stoppard has returned to *Hamlet* and has produced a reworking so condensed as to make Marowitz's version seem prolix and conservative. Stoppard's new *Hamlet*, originally designed for performance on a bus, is now the second half of the first part of *Dogg's Hamlet, Cahoot's Macbeth* (1979), a set of linked plays every bit as extraordinary as its extraordinary title.

Dogg's Hamlet is set in a school somewhere in England: at least an audience will assume that the school is English because its headmaster, Professor Dogg, has ordered building materials from Leamington Spa (which here serves as the prototype of a standard British town of comic normality). It is the school speech-day; there is to be a prize-giving, and afterwards the pupils are to perform *Hamlet*. Nothing could be more English, nothing more invitingly normal than this: it is the stuff of a thousand English comedies. But the schoolboys, their headmaster, his wife, and the lady who is to present the prizes speak an extraordinary language (known as Dogg). Dogg and English have a common word-hoard, but attach different meanings to their shared vocables (for instance the numbers *one* to *ten* in Dogg are: sun, dock, trog, slack, pan, sock, slight, bright, none, tun). There arrives from Leamington an English-speaking lorry-driver, delivering materials with which to build a platform for the prize-giving: he can neither understand nor be understood, and there is great confusion and some violence of a minor sort (chiefly caused by the inconvenient fact that 'Useless, git [term of abuse]' in Dogg means 'Good day, sir' in English). Eventually the platform is built; the prize-giving takes place; and *Hamlet* is performed – twice: once in a fifteen-minute version and then as an encore in under two minutes.

Cahoot's Macbeth, the second half of Stoppard's double-bill, has a different setting. Here we are to watch *Macbeth* being performed in someone's living room. (Stoppard, after visiting Czechoslovakia in 1977, learned that certain actors – among them the playwright Pavel Kohout – having been prevented from acting by the state authorities had taken to giving illicit performances of *Macbeth* in flats in Prague.) The play proceeds normally, though in a highly condensed version, until a police inspector bursts into the room. Despite his wise-cracking manner (by a horrible irony it is this policeman who provides the evening's comic relief) he threatens the actors with arrest and imprisonment for acting without authority. Performing Shakespeare without state approval, he explains, is simply a way of ignoring and thus of undermining the authority of the state. He also makes it clear that he is prepared, with official connivance, to twist the language of the statute-books to any length in order to get a conviction. (Of the words of one statute he argues: 'Who's to say what was meant? Words can be your friend or your enemy, depending on who's throwing the book, so watch your language' (p. 59). These are the crucial words in Stoppard's play and the key to his purposes.) Having taken everyone's name and address the inspector leaves for a short while, but within a few moments a second interruption occurs when the lorry-driver from *Dogg's Hamlet* enters the room. Once again he has driven from Leamington (his last speech in the play suggests that it has been a long drive) and once again he is trying to deliver building materials. But there is a difference: now he too speaks Dogg and soon all of the actors performing *Macbeth* begin to speak it also. The inspector calls again, to complete his work of harassment, and is the only one unable to understand what is being said. In response he becomes increasingly frustrated and threatening ('If it's not free expression, I don't know what is' (p. 75). This is an irony, since he certainly does not know what free expression is.) The performance ends in manic confusion – the lorry-driver building yet another platform; the actors spouting *Macbeth* entirely in Dogg language; the inspector piling building material of his own between them and their audience. The last (suitably ambiguous) words go to the lorry-driver: 'But I should be back by Tuesday'. Is this the cry of the expatriate Briton seeking to return to his beloved Leamington, where policemen know their place, and where that place is neither the theatre nor the best living-rooms? Or are they words meaning heaven-only-knows-what in Dogg?

This is an odd play certainly, but, with Stoppard, it is wise to assume that the odder the play is the better it will be. There are, indeed, solid reasons for thinking *Dogg's Hamlet, Cahoot's Macbeth* better than *Rosencrantz and Guildenstern are Dead* despite the earlier play's far greater acclaim. In particular the later play is much the more economical, with none of that freewheeling discussion of whatever interested Stoppard at the time that so much disfigures parts of *Rosencrantz and Guildenstern are Dead.* Yet it is precisely in relation to economy, considered as a dramatic virtue, that we need to raise a fundamental question about *Dogg's Hamlet, Cahoot's Macbeth.* Why are we treated to a shortened version of *Hamlet*? There is no obvious answer. The first part of *Dogg's Hamlet* introduces us to Dogg-language; we need to know about this language in order to follow the last part of *Cahoot's Macbeth.* The schoolboys' *Hamlet*, however, is performed throughout in English; a lady in the audience shouts 'Marmalade' at one point – roughly the equivalent of 'Bravo' – but that is the only irruption of Dogg into the piece.

When we learn that the shortened *Hamlet* existed earlier as a separate project we may begin to suspect that Stoppard has simply rough-stitched it in place in order to make a longer play. He is quite capable of such outrages: *New-Found-Land* is an extremely long and extravagant soliloquy arbitrarily punched into the middle of *Dirty Linen* (1976). Moreover, considered in isolation, Stoppard's fifteen-minute *Hamlet* is not very interesting; it lacks Marowitz's fire, and perhaps simply reminds us that, though you need talent and energy to write a play, you need only a pair of scissors to cut one. But if we put the shortened *Hamlet* back into the context which Stoppard has provided for it and consider it in relation to *Dogg's Hamlet, Cahoot's Macbeth* as a whole we can begin to see why it is where it is and why it must be there.

Stoppard begins our evening with a lesson in Dogg-language. He then gives us a Shakespeare play (*Hamlet*), an interval, another Shakespeare play (*Macbeth*), and a final burst of Dogg-language. Our evening thus has a V-shaped structure; its second part is the mirror image of its first. The lorry-driver speaks English in the first half, Dogg in the second; ordinary conversation is carried on in Dogg in the first, in English in the second half; Shakespeare is perfomed in English in the first, but (eventually) in Dogg in the second. These common elements differently arranged create a far-reaching difference in mood. The first part is set in a school, and Dogg, though a serious language to those who speak it, has for an audience the air of an extended schoolboy-joke; a language in which you may safely greet your headmaster with the words 'Useless, git' is every schoolboy's dream. Within this innocent world Shakespeare's plays are performed by amateurs to whom his words are a foreign language. They perform him badly to dutiful applause – but they perform him without danger. The only one at risk in this production is Shakespeare himself, his longest play despatched in two minutes flat.

In *Cahoot's Macbeth* innocence has been lost and everything is darker in consequence. Shakespeare is being performed by professionals, men and women to whom an overweening state denies access to their legitimate rewards. He is being performed, furthermore, by men and women who stand in the very greatest danger. Their attitude towards what they are doing is thoroughly workmanlike, for putting on Shakespeare's plays is their trade. They do not perform his works because they believe them to contain insights without which the world must remain forever blind: they perform him because they have been told not to do so. Their performances to a frightened handful of spectators are acts of defiance that are the essential constituents of freedom. (Their spokesman is forced to say: 'I'm afraid the performance is not open to the public' – p. 56.) But their plight, as Stoppard presents it, and his presentation humanises their plight, is that they are workmen denied gainful employment, tradesmen denied access to their trade. It is as though Stoppard is commenting on, and revoking, an earlier witticism – 'We're *actors*, we're the opposite of people' – spoken by the Player in *Rosencrantz and Guildenstern are Dead* (p. 47).

Finding themselves in their conflict with the inspector in a world in which language is flexible though party attitudes are not, the actors take refuge in a linguistic evasion, finishing their play in a language (it really is the language of freedom) which the inspector cannot understand but whose rhythms are recognisably those of *Macbeth*. Stoppard's play ends with this small triumph for the actors, but it also ends, as any play true to the facts of state repression must, with the police inspector, instrument of that repression, ridiculous but still menacing and undefeated.

Comedy or tragedy?

What sort of play is *Rosencrantz and Guildenstern are Dead*? Is it a comedy? Or a tragedy? Or the sort of play that cannot properly be described as either the one thing or the other? Most people who go to see it do so expecting that they will be made to laugh: by reputation the play is a comedy, though (as many who have seen it would wish to add) it is a comedy freighted with sadness.

Judging whether a play is comic or tragic by how audiences answer simple questions (Did you laugh? Did you cry?) has not seemed to most theorists of the drama a very satisfactory way of proceeding, and from the earliest times attempts have been made at distinguishing between comedy and tragedy on principle. The Greek philosopher and critic Aristotle (384–322BC), in his *De Poetica*, sought, for example, to define tragedy as drama in which spectators are moved to pity and fear by watching enacted before them the misfortunes suffered by a man (neither vicious nor depraved, and of high social standing) because of some 'error of judgement' on his part.* Though Aristotle is certainly not denying the emotional impact of tragedy – that it produces pity and fear is an essential element in his account of it – it is, nevertheless, in his view the *fall* of the tragic hero which prompts us to feel these emotions: plot, he says, is 'the first and the most important thing in Tragedy'. We decide whether a play is tragic or not by looking at the curve of its plot.

Unfortunately the second book of the *De Poetica*, in which Aristotle discussed comedy, is lost, and what he might there have said has to be guessed at from hints thrown out elsewhere. He seems to have believed that comedy shows us men who, unlike tragic heroes, are worse than the average man through their possession of bad qualities (greed, cupidity, unseemly doting upon young girls) which we may properly ridicule. Later amplifiers of his account have sometimes thought that comedy, in Aristotle's view, is a moral enterprise which exalts virtue by ridiculing those vices which are appropriately ridiculed: a play which ridiculed misfortune that was unrelated to vice or that was far in excess of the vice to which it was related, would be cruel rather than comic. At one point,

**The Works of Aristotle*, edited by J. A. Smith, W. D. Ross *et al*, 12 volumes, Clarendon Press, Oxford, 1908–52, vol. XI.

however, Aristotle argues that comedy may be distinguished from tragedy by a mechanical examination of its plot, for he writes of one tragedy that it has a subplot which 'belongs rather to Comedy' since it shows the bitterest enemies 'walking off good friends at the end, with no slaying of any one by any one'.

What emerges with great clarity from the foregoing account is that in Aristotelian terms *Rosencrantz and Guildenstern are Dead* is neither a tragedy nor a comedy. Rosencrantz and Guildenstern are incompetent, unfortunate, and all at sea (Stoppard's Act 3 makes this last point in visual terms): to ridicule them would be cruel. But, on the other hand, they do not have the stature of tragic heroes; nor is it easy to see of what error of judgement they are guilty. Their view of their condition is partial certainly: they never know that they are characters in a play, nor (unlike their audience) do they have any knowledge of Shakespeare's *Hamlet*. But how could they be told that they are characters in a play? They cannot leave the play in order to look down upon it from the outside, and any message brought to them within the play they interpret, reasonably enough, as just another particle of experience, indistinguishable from the other particles of experience which make up their lives. They are, in short, the victims of ineradicable ignorance; but, if they are indeed victims, in what sense may they be considered guilty?

In the Middle Ages there emerged a simpler view of the distinction between comedy and tragedy than that given by Aristotle. We decide whether a play is the one thing or the other solely by looking at what happens at its close: comedies end in marriage, tragedies in death. It is the view to which Stoppard's Player subscribes wholeheartedly: 'Tragedy, sir. Deaths and disclosures' (p. 17). On this view *Rosencrantz and Guildenstern are Dead* is a tragedy. This conclusion, however, conflicts both with the expectation of the modern playgoer and with his experience.

Perhaps the problem of deciding what sort of play Stoppard has written is compounded for us by our having unduly restricted the number of categories to which it may be assigned. There is precedent within *Hamlet* itself, which can never be far from our minds, for a generous expansion of the available categories: 'tragedy, comedy, history, pastoral, . . . tragical-historical, tragical-comical-historical-pastoral' (II.2.390). But this list, put together by the gabbling Polonius, is too generous: it madly divides and proliferates genres until a point is reached where, though the compound term may *describe* a play admirably, it ceases to be able to *classify* it. If we worked in the spirit of Polonius we should end up having to argue, almost scene by scene, that a play is tragic here, but comic there, occasionally pastoral (sometimes when comic, and sometimes when tragic), and in parts historical as well.

We appear to have reached an impasse, and yet there is a way forward along the least auspicious path. Tragedies end in death; comedies in marriage. Tragedies simply end (they are, Aristotle says, imitations 'of a *complete* action'); comedies end in new beginnings. Marriage implies children, and children repeat the pattern of their parents' lives, begetting in their turn children who repeat the pattern once again. Comedy, in short, is cyclical.

At one point in Act 3 Rosencrantz and Guildenstern are debating whether to tell Hamlet of Claudius's plans to murder him:

> ROS: We're his *friends.*
> GUIL: How do you know?
> ROS: From our young days brought up with him.
> GUIL: You've only got their word for it.
> ROS: But that's what we depend on.
> GUIL: Well, yes, and then again no.
>
> (pp. 82–3)

'Yes, and then again no': it will be to our advantage if we can acquire a little of Guildenstern's nicely judged scepticism when we try to answer the following fundamental question – how do we know that Rosencrantz and Guildenstern die at the end of Stoppard's play? Because of the play's title? But how do we know that the title is telling us the truth? Because they die in Shakespeare's play? But Stoppard's play is not Shakespeare's, and Stoppard's Rosencrantz and Guildenstern are not Shakespeare's Rosencrantz and Guildenstern precisely because *Stoppard's Rosencrantz and Guildenstern are characters in Shakespeare's play whereas Shakespeare's Rosencrantz and Guildenstern are not*. There is a paradox here, and one which is remarkably difficult to spell out, but it is Stoppard's founding paradox upon which he constructs the entire edifice of *Rosencrantz and Guildenstern are Dead.*

Shakespeare's *Hamlet* purports to be a representation of occurrences in the real world: whether those events really happened or are known to be fictional does not, in respect of the present argument, matter at all. Shakespeare's Rosencrantz and Guildenstern are presented to us as though they are real courtiers, set real tasks by a real king. Of course in one sense (it is common sense) they *are* characters in a play, but that is not how Shakespeare presents them. With Stoppard's Rosencrantz and Guildenstern the case is quite different: doubtless they think they are real human beings, and they have not read the play in which they have such minor parts, but nevertheless it is as characters in that play that they are presented to us. (This point is sometimes easier to understand if we think in visual terms. A picture of a tree is not a tree, but neither is it the picture of a picture of a tree. Shakespeare's Rosencrantz and Guildenstern are pictures of real people; Stoppard's are pictures of pictures.) Stoppard's purport is thus radically different from

Shakespeare's. In the sense indicated above Shakespeare's Rosencrantz and Guildenstern are really people, who really die. But Stoppard's Rosencrantz and Guildenstern are characters in a play. Can characters in a play really die? Consider the following exchange between Guildenstern and the Player:

GUIL: Aren't you going to – come *on*?
PLAYER: I *am* on.
GUIL: But if you *are* on, you can't *come* on. *Can* you?

(p. 25)

A similar argument applies to death. You cannot die unless you have first been alive. Can characters in a play really be said to be alive? A character is only a plan: certain words in a certain order, delivered in a certain tone of voice, and with certain accompanying gestures and movements. The plan is realised in performance, whether by an actor or by a reader, and the character may then be said to 'come alive': once the realisation is over we might even agree to say that the character is dead. This is a highly metaphorical death, however, and furthermore applies to all characters in a play whether or not they represent someone who dies. And it is a death from whose grip the character is resurrected at the next performance. By changing the status of Shakespeare's characters, by making Rosencrantz and Guildenstern characters in a play who really are characters in a play, Stoppard has denied them access to all save this metaphorical death. He has made their lot inescapably cyclical.

ROS: Is he dead?
PLAYER: Who knows?
GUIL (*rattled*): He's not coming back?
PLAYER: Hardly.
ROS: He's dead then.

(p. 90)

Guildenstern returns to the point very near the end of the play: death, he reflects, is 'the endless time of never coming back' (p. 95). But that it is a point that does not apply to him is made clear by his very last words: 'Well, we'll know better next time. Now you see me, now you —— (*And disappears*).'

In the 1967 version the cyclical nature of the play was still more obvious: perhaps, indeed, it was altered because it was too obvious. A messenger bangs upon a door and calls out two names. The next performance is about to begin (like Beauchamp's loop of tape in Stoppard's radio play *Artist Descending a Staircase* (broadcast 1972): 'this entire sequence begins again'). There will be no better luck next time, for Rosencrantz and Guildenstern are as firmly fixed into their text as is the coin that comes down heads ninety-two times. The title deceives us: Rosencrantz and Guildenstern are not dead. Theirs is no tragedy – the play in which they are trapped is remorselessly cyclical, and is, as no one has seriously doubted, a comedy of sorts, though heavy with inevitable sadness: 'so shall you hear of carnal, bloody and unnatural acts, of accidental judgments, casual slaughters, of deaths put on by cunning and forced cause, and . . . . purposes mistook fallen on the inventors' heads.'

Part 4

Hints for study

Getting to know the play

Getting to know a novel or a poem is so much a matter of reading and re-reading the text that people often assume that the text *is* the novel or poem. But the text of a play is not the play itself, since most plays, and certainly *Rosencrantz and Guildenstern are Dead* falls within this category, are designed to be seen in performance. Of course plays designed for reading rather than for acting have been written by poets and novelists, but Stoppard is not a poet or novelist who also writes plays: he is first and last a man whose natural medium is the *theatre* – and a theatre, as the Greek origins of the word put beyond doubt, is a place where people go to *see* things. Only in performance are the differences between Rosencrantz and Guildenstern readily apparent; in reading the play to yourself, particularly in reading those sections which consist of the rapid exchange of short speeches, it is easy to lose track of who is speaking to whom. Though a part of Stoppard's point is that Rosencrantz and Guildenstern are not easily told apart, their complete fusion into one which can easily occur in single-person reading, especially silent reading, does not suit his purposes at all. In a stage performance such a fusion and confusion could only occur if a director had identical twins in his company and were perverse enough to use them and to dress them identically. (It will be worth your considering here whether you agree that a director would be wrong to use identical twins, identically costumed. Which arguments in favour of and which against the practice would you assemble? Consider, for instance, the effect of that scene, pp. 34–5, in which Rosencrantz cannot remember whether his name is Rosencrantz or Guildenstern, upon spectators who cannot tell the actors apart. Furthermore, how well would Stoppard's very slight characterisation, his making Rosencrantz more stupid than his friend but also a bit nicer, stand up in such circumstances?)

Rosencrantz and Guildenstern are Dead is often performed by college students (it is a play in which very young actors may take all of the parts without incongruity of effect) and by amateurs generally. Nevertheless the chances are high that most people who study the play, and this is very true of those studying abroad, will not have had an opportunity of seeing it on stage. What is to be done?

Though some study, concentrated revision for instance, is a solitary activity most is not, and indeed study of the drama is often best when it is most sociable. Very few students need to study alone; it should be possible for most readers of the play to get together with others in order to stage, in however elementary a fashion, their own performance. (Remember that if your performance is a public one you must obtain the permission of Mr Stoppard's agents. You will find their names printed on the back of the title-page of your edition of the play.) Even a simple reading round the class will serve to clarify matters greatly, but it is better to try to achieve a 'proper' performance, in which actors move about within a designated play-area. Such a performance need not be at all elaborate: a very basic version can be staged with only three actors – one will be Rosencrantz, one Guildenstern, and the third will have to be everyone else. If more actors are available they can easily be fitted into a performance (as additional courtiers and attendants if no speaking parts are available: in the play's first professional production more than twenty-five actors were used, many of whom can have had nothing to say). More elaborate still would be a performance with a stage-set and costumes. The construction and making of these will also serve to increase your knowledge of the play and make use of the talents of those students, often among the best, who find acting a burden.

Above all, throughout the process of putting on the play, actors, extras, and stage-hands should be encouraged to talk about what they are doing. If they are encouraged then interesting questions, of far-reaching significance, will often be raised in the most casual manner. Perhaps you have more actresses than actors in your class and want to give some of the men's parts over to women; but should you, as has happened in at least one amateur production, allow Alfred to be played by a girl? Whether or not a polished performance is the result of all these deliberations is of no great moment: what matters is the increased likelihood of everyone's seeing the play not as marks upon a page but as spoken words, as movements across a stage, as first one grouping of actors and then as another. What may well have seemed merely dull in reading (the opening scene, for instance) will suddenly take on life: what had seemed insignificant will be found to have point and purpose; stage-directions, which in a printed version are a part of the text itself, will disappear in order to carry out their silent task of marshalling the action.

A few students, because of the time at which they are obliged to study of because of the remoteness of their homes, may be unable to join with others in this sort of activity. Even they, however, must not rest content with a simple reading of the play. At the very least they should read it aloud, seriously attending to variations in emphasis and intonation as they do so (Stoppard's stage-directions are useful in this respect). A better idea is to construct a simple model theatre (it need be nothing more difficult to obtain than a table-top) within which figures can be moved about. Such a model, though a poor substitute for seeing the play in a performance, will allow it to be experienced as a series of happenings in space as well as in time, for it is the spatial aspect of theatre which a mere reading of a text, however patient that reading may be, cannot suggest adequately. If a model theatre and toy actors smack uncomfortably of playing with dolls, you might comfort yourself by trying to consider how well this image of a doll that is played with by a force which it is powerless to resist sums up what is happening in Stoppard's own play – itself, as the preceding notes will have made clear, a work for the theatre that never forgets that a play is a game and that *homo sapiens* is *homo ludens*.

A note on examinations

The essential point to be made about examinations, at whatever level you encounter them, is that they are best regarded as the natural conclusion to a course of study. A question on *Rosencrantz and Guildenstern are Dead* is designed to test the quality of your understanding of the play, developed over a long period of time. It is not designed to allow you to display how much of the text you have managed to commit to memory in the preceding few days.

Preparing for an examination is not a special sort of activity, undertaken after you have finished reading Stoppard's plays and no longer have to think about them. Preparation, moreover, is not an activity that you should confine to the last few weeks or days of your academic term. Above all, those frenzied last-minute revision stints which so many students inflict upon themselves are best avoided. All save the most aggressively competitive students are likely to be harmed by them, and they frequently destroy all hope of a student's ever again enjoying the work upon which he is being examined. In English studies the mere swot is at a disadvantage. There are no formulas to be learned, or lists of irregular verbs to be mastered, and committing to memory a few striking scenes or snatches of dialogue, though sometimes a useful revision exercise, is not sufficient to guarantee success in an examination.

This last point needs to be looked at more carefully since many students think that an examination is designed to test their knowledge of an author, and think in addition that 'knowing an author' equals 'being able to recite the words that he has written'. An examination, however, is properly designed to test the *quality* of your understanding of an author's work, and merely reciting his words, however accurately, will not satisfy the requirements of such a test. What matters is whether the words which you cite support and illustrate and help to advance your argument. If they do not do so they are irrelevant, and ought not to be included. It is within the examination room itself that you will need to recollect those parts of Stoppard's play that are relevant to your answer: the danger in learning lists of quotations by heart a few days before the examination is that you will include them in your answer merely because you know them, without regard to their relevance.

Many students, who in the ordinary course of events have no difficulty in thinking clearly on quite complex matters, are nevertheless worried when they are told that they will have to think during an examination. This worry frequently leads them into the grip of one of the unhappiest of all malpractices: question-spotting. Reading past examination papers in order to see what sort of questions are likely to be set is a wise use of your time, but do not forget that you are sitting this year's examination, not last year's. Your examiners have the right to set questions which they think proper and the duty to avoid setting questions which simply reproduce those of former years. Examinations test your responsiveness to the question that is in front of you; your ability to answer last year's question will impress no one. Never prepare answers in advance.

What lies behind question-spotting and answering in advance is the fear which many students have that under examination pressure their minds will go blank as soon as they put pen to paper. For most students, however, there is no real danger that this will happen provided that preparation has been thorough, relaxed, and of the right kind. Such preparation takes time and cannot be hurried but since it is indistinguishable from a serious and interested study of your text, whether in the library or in the theatre, it is pleasurable and rewarding in itself, quite apart from the benefits which it confers in the examination room.

Preparing and presenting an essay

It is probably fair to assume that most readers of *Rosencrantz and Guildenstern are Dead* who are working to acquire academic qualifications will at some time be asked to write at least one essay of about fifteen hundred words. A week or a fortnight will be given for the completion of the task and direct access to the principal text and to secondary authorities will not be prohibited. What preparation does such an essay require? How is it to be written? What should it contain?

We may usefully begin by distinguishing between general preparedness and special preparations. Having read the play carefully several times, having seen it staged, or having taken part in it (as outlined above) will result in most students being generally prepared to write an essay. Sometimes such general preparedness is all that is required. Usually, however, an essay question will invite consideration of specific aspects of the play that may have escaped the attention of even a well-prepared student. In these circumstances it is best to read the play once again, with the question firmly in mind, carefully noting incidents and speeches and turns of phrase that will be *relevant* to an answer.

Many students have great difficulty in distinguishing what is relevant from what is not, and yet, in the vast majority of cases, all that is needed in making the distinction is a little common sense. The clue to what is relevant is usually contained in the question itself. For example: 'Assess the influence of Samuel Beckett upon Stoppard, with special reference to *Rosencrantz and Guildenstern are Dead* and *Waiting for Godot*' (which like many essay 'questions' is not, strictly speaking, a question at all) invites discussion of Beckett's influence upon Stoppard. It does not invite you to discuss, however enticing the topic may seem to be, the extent or nature of Shakespeare's influence. If a reference to Shakespeare is to appear in an essay produced in response to this question it should do so only in passing. A useful way of mentioning him, without wasting time and without losing sight of what is principally required, is by means of such an opening sentence as: 'Although Stoppard's indebtedness to Shakespeare is both obvious and wide-ranging throughout *Rosencrantz and Guildenstern are Dead*, of great significance also (though less obvious, and more difficult to assess) is the influence of Samuel Beckett.'

Different people will answer the same question in different ways and there are often legitimate differences of opinion over what a good answer should contain. There is, however, broad agreement among markers over what an essay should *not* contain. Bear the following points in mind:

(*a*) Very few questions (and no good ones) require a student simply to tell again in his own words the plot of a play. Use plot summary sparingly and only when the question cannot be answered without such summary.

(*b*) Quotations from primary material (from the text of Stoppard's play and from any other play with which you are comparing it) should usually be brief and ought only to be included when they have a definite part in forwarding the argument of your essay. Decorative quotations, introduced merely to indicate your knowledge of the text, should be avoided.

(*c*) When deciding whether or not to include quotations from secondary material (from books or articles about Stoppard) the most stringent tests of relevance should be applied.

(*d*) When you introduce your chosen quotation avoid hackneyed formulas: 'As Professor *Blank* has said in his stimulating/

penetrating/important study of ....' Secondary authorities frequently set a bad example themselves in this respect.

(*e*) Choose observations that are worthy of quotation. Do not, for instance, write: 'As Professor *Blank* has reminded us, "William Shakespeare is the greatest influence on Stoppard's *Rosencrantz and Guildenstern are Dead*" .' *Blank* may very well be correct, but he will not thank you (nor will anyone else) for granting prominence to such perfectly routine observations.

(*f*) Do not quote what you do not understand, and never fall into the trap of supposing that it must be worth quoting *because* you do not understand it. Not all academic authors write clearly or well: there is no advantage to be gained from solemnly introducing into your essay material which will disfigure it while its presence there will call your own good judgement into question.

(*g*) Direct use of secondary material (quotation) must always be acknowledged directly. In a classroom essay the author's name, the title of the book, and a page reference should follow the quotation in parentheses. Failure to acknowledge quotations, and, worse still, failure to indicate that they are quotations, is a serious matter which often leads to an essay being rejected in its entirety. Indirect use of secondary material should also be acknowledged – by means of a list of 'Books Used' (avoid 'Bibliography', a pompous and inaccurate term in this context) at the end of your essay. Where the details or direction of an argument, though not the wording itself, are borrowed from another author specific acknowledgement of the borrowing is proper and in more advanced essay work it is essential. In short, acknowledge indebtedness openly, but do not confuse the nervous accumulation of secondary authorities with sound scholarship.

Some trial questions

1. '*Rosencrantz and Guildenstern are Dead* is a play which has its greatest impact in performance.' Discuss.
2. Outline the influence of Samuel Beckett's *Waiting for Godot* upon Stoppard's *Rosencrantz and Guildenstern are Dead.* (Younger students should note that they are unlikely to encounter this question, or one like it, unless *Waiting for Godot* is another of their set texts.)
3. 'Slightly literate music-hall perhaps' is Stoppard's own description of *Rosencrantz and Guildenstern are Dead.* Is it a good description?
4. Outline the relationship between 'enjoying Stoppard's plays' and 'taking them seriously'.
5. 'All the world's a stage, and all the men and women merely players.'

Comparisons of the world to the theatre are part of a very ancient tradition. What use does Stoppard make of such comparisons?

6. Why do you think that Stoppard chose to attach his play to *Hamlet* rather than, for example, to *Timon of Athens* or *Coriolanus* or *King Lear*?
7. Describe the main differences between Shakespeare's use of the English language and Stoppard's, paying particular attention to those scenes in *Rosencrantz and Guildenstern are Dead* in which *Hamlet* is extensively quoted.
8. 'Much of our pleasure in comedy comes directly from our sense of the artist at work; much of our attention is directly fixed upon the dramatist as well as upon his characters.'

   Discuss with reference to Stoppard's *Rosencrantz and Guildenstern are Dead.*
9. Has your reading of Stoppard's play enriched your understanding of *Hamlet*?

A specimen essay

'*Rosencrantz and Guildenstern are Dead* is a play which has its greatest impact in performance.' Discuss.

Most novels invite us to consider people in relation to each other and rely upon a precise use of words in order to describe or illustrate such relationships. The dramatist relies upon a precise use of words too, but he has at this disposal resources that are unavailable to the novelist. Of these much the most potent is the physical presence of the actor. The bodies of great actors are eloquent even when they are standing still (there are so many ways of standing still), and when they move they give graphic expression to those relationships which the dramatist seeks to illuminate. We frequently speak of art as being 'moving': we mean that whatever art we are considering (a symphony, a painting, a novel, poem, or play) has a powerful emotional effect upon us. 'Moving' here is a metaphor, but one reason why the drama is so frequently moving in this sense is that it is the art medium in which physical movement plays so large a part.

'Actions speak louder than words' we often say: good dramatists know this and seek to employ gesture and posture and position as carefully as they employ words, for together words and actions can have an impact greater than either can have alone. Here, for instance, is a passage from the opening scene of *Rosencrantz and Guildenstern are Dead* in which Guildenstern and Rosencrantz are betting upon the toss of a coin:

GUIL: Your capacity for trust made me wonder if perhaps . . . you, alone . . . . . (*He turns on him suddenly, reaches out a hand.*) Touch. (ROS *clasps his hand.* GUIL *pulls him up to him.*) (*More intensely.*): We have been spinning coins together since – (*He releases him almost as violently.*) This is not the first time we have spun coins! (p. 10)

Even in reading this passage we may find it moving, but its true effectiveness is only to be experienced in performance. The rows of dots, for example, which in reading indicate a pause are in performance the pauses themselves. The stage-directions become actions not words, and the simple contact of hand and hand is there for all to witness – a universal symbol of friendship (we speak of 'hands across the sea') which is also a universal example of friendliness. The whole incident is 'touching' – another word which, like 'moving', describes the world of our emotions in terms derived from the world of action.

Though more delicate than many others this not the only instance of Stoppard's employing action to great effect. Only at the end, when they go to their deaths, do Rosencrantz and Guildenstern manage to leave the stage. They are prisoners in Shakespeare's plot, condemned to tread the boards as prisoners tread a wheel; their freedom is physically proscribed in a way to which words alone cannot give adequate expression. Immediately after Claudius tells them to seek out Hamlet and recover the body of Polonius (p. 65) Stoppard shows us that they are prisoners by the way in which he has them move about the stage, pacing its edges but never crossing them. They march, full of resolve (they march; they do not walk), to opposite ends of the stage; their resolve collapses; they halt; they march towards each other; they halt; they wheel around, and march, and halt, and wheel, and march, and halt again. They dance out their confinement, or sculpt it in air by the motions of their limbs, and we see them doing it. 'Seeing is believing' we say; no one ever says 'reading is believing'.

Words, too, are actions, not just meanings. When we speak them we give physical expression to them: they are sound-waves passing through the air. Consider the following passage, typical of many in the play. Rosencrantz and Guildenstern toy with the idea of removing the Player's ability to give physical expression to his words:

GUIL: So you've caught up.
PLAYER (*coldly*): Not yet, sir.
GUIL: Now mind your tongue, or we'll have it out and throw the rest of you away, like a nightingale at a Roman feast.
ROS: Took the very words out of my mouth.
GUIL: You'd be *lost* for words.
ROS: You'd be tongue-tied.

Certainly a reader faced with the whole passage (pp. 45–6; only a third of it is quoted here) might well wonder, taking his cue from the passage itself, whether it might not profitably be cut. In silent reading, two voices reduced to one, the passage is sluggish, but in performance, spoken at top speed with admonitory and near-hysterical stabbings-forward of the finger, these words are physical weapons of assault.

The dramatist's medium is not words alone (a play is not a poem) but words spoken by people who move about upon a stage. *Rosencrantz and Guildenstern are Dead* has its greatest impact in performance because only in performance is it presented to us in the medium for which it was conceived.

A specimen examination answer

Outline the influence of Samuel Beckett's *Waiting for Godot* on Stoppard's *Rosencrantz and Guildenstern are Dead.*

Stoppard, both when being interviewed and in his plays themselves, has admitted an indebtedness to Samuel Beckett. Nowhere is this indebtedness more readily apparent than in *Rosencrantz and Guildenstern are Dead.*

Waiting for Godot is a tragicomedy (Beckett's own description of it) in which two characters, Vladimir and Estragon, spend the whole of the day, as they must spend the whole of their lives, waiting for the mysterious Godot. Unlike characters in the conventional well-made play, Vladimir and Estragon tell us very little about themselves (indeed they seem to know very little about themselves). Their speeches are short (many are fewer than ten words long) and Beckett does not seek to give them easily identifiable speech traits. Their situation is obscure: each evening upon an open road near a tree they wait for Godot, whom they have probably never met (the *certainty* that they have never met is denied them: 'he's a kind of acquaintance . . . we hardly know him . . . we don't know him very well . . . I wouldn't even know him if I saw him'). They more than half-suspect that he will never come to meet them, or that they will miss him, and that their waiting will have been in vain. They wait upon a stage (Beckett never seeks to pretend that it is not a stage) fighting off boredom by playing games: their cross-talk, so much a feature of the play and one which Stoppard freely adopts, is a sort of game; they call each other insulting names, half in earnest and half in jest; they fool about with their hats in an ancient circus-clown routine; they pretend to be other people; they flirt with suicide. But all the time they seek to pass the time – representatives of a humanity which waits, half-afraid that the end will come, half-afraid that it will not.

As this summary suggests, there is much in common between

Stoppard's play and Beckett's. Rosencrantz and Guildenstern are two Elizabethans passing the time in a place without any visible character. They too speak short speeches, are not easily told apart, play games to idle away the time, banter ceaselessly, and rely on the entrance of others upon the stage for both amusement and impetus. And it is not only in their relationship to their basic situation that Rosencrantz and Guildenstern resemble Vladimir and Estragon: they resemble them also in their relationship with one another – each partner in both pairs is at once carping and conciliatory, for partner is tied to partner in an interdependency that admits of friction but not of fracture.

Both pairs wait in imperfect awareness of what goes on, and both wait upon the boards of a public stage. Stoppard has borrowed (the borrowings are so explicit that they must be an allusion) Vladimir's and Estragon's references both to the boredom of their situation, which is also their audience's boredom ('This is becoming really insignificant'), and to the physical presence of the audience (Estragon looks out at them: 'inspiring prospects', he mutters. The auditorium is 'that bog').

Rosencrantz and Guildenstern are Dead and *Waiting for Godot* are related: that much is demonstrable. But the nature of the relationship is not so easily established. However, one thing is certain: Stoppard is no more trying to repeat Beckett's play than he is trying to repeat Shakespeare's. *Waiting for Godot* is a tragicomedy; *Rosencrantz and Guildenstern are Dead* is not. Both dramatists, in providing their moving-pictures of the world, repeat the ancient comparison of world and theatre ('All the world's a stage') but Stoppard, by means of a device that carefully preserves his play's comic standing, gives to his audience an advantage which Beckett, in every way the sterner playwright, denies to his. We know *Hamlet*, but we do not know who Godot is (God perhaps, or Death perhaps, but whatever we think Godot is we have to add 'perhaps'). And Stoppard brings his play to its close with a theatrical flourish that the austerer Beckett will never allow. Rosencrantz and Guildenstern live on in ceaseless repetition, born again at the start of each performance. And yet each performance, though a foregone conclusion (there will be no 'better luck next time'), is for them a fresh start; for Vladimir and Estragon, in contrast, there are no fresh starts – indeed no fresh anything: one has feet that smell, the other breath that stinks. Day follows day, each one like all the others in every essential respect, distinct enough only to confirm and strengthen its inescapable boredom. Vladimir and Estragon live out their whole lives in paralysed anticipation of what, if it comes, they may not even recognise. 'We learn something every day, to our cost', the Player tells Rosencrantz and Guildenstern in Stoppard's comedy: if that line had appeared in Beckett's tragicomedy we should not so easily have put it laughingly to one side.

Part 5

Suggestions for further reading

The text

The text of the play referred to in these Notes is:

Rosencrantz and Guildenstern are Dead, Faber & Faber, London, 1967; revised edition 1968.

Other works by Stoppard

Only works to which reference is made in these Notes are listed here. Dates are those of publication and may differ from the dates of first performance.

Lord Malquist and Mr Moon, Faber & Faber, London and Boston, 1974; first published by Anthony Blond, London, 1966.

The Real Inspector Hound, Faber & Faber, London, 1968.

Jumpers, Faber & Faber, London, 1972.

Artist Descending a Staircase and *Where Are They Now?*, Faber & Faber, London, 1973.

Travesties, Faber & Faber, London and Boston, 1975.

Dirty Linen and *New-Found-Land*, Faber & Faber, London and Boston, 1976.

Night and Day, Faber & Faber, London and Boston, 1978.

Every Good Boy Deserves Favour and *Professional Foul*, Faber & Faber, London and Boston, 1978.

Dogg's Hamlet, Cahoot's Macbeth, Faber & Faber, London and Boston, 1979.

Undiscovered Country, Faber & Faber, London and Boston, 1980.

On the Razzle, Faber & Faber, London and Boston, 1981.

Other primary texts

BECKETT, SAMUEL: *Waiting for Godot*, Faber & Faber, London, 1956.

GILBERT, WILLIAM SCHWENCK: *Original Plays*, 3rd series, Chatto & Windus, London, 1928 (includes *Rosencrantz and Guildenstern*)

GILBERT, WILLIAM SCHWENCK: *Plays by W.S. Gilbert*, edited by George Rowell, Cambridge University Press, Cambridge, 1982 (also includes *Rosencrantz and Guildenstern*).

MAROWITZ, CHARLES: *The Marowitz Shakespeare*, Marion Boyars, London, 1978 (includes Marowitz's version of *Hamlet*).

SHAKESPEARE, WILLIAM: *Hamlet*, edited by Harold Jenkins, The Arden Edition of the Works of William Shakespeare, Methuen, London and New York, 1982.

Criticism

BENNETT, JONATHAN: 'Philosophy and Mr Stoppard', in *Philosophy: The Journal of the Royal Institute of Philosophy*, 50 (1975), 5–18. An excellent article by a professional philosopher who admires *Rosencrantz and Guildenstern are Dead* but who thinks *Jumpers* philosophically slapdash, superficial and muddled.

BIGSBY, C. W. E.: *Tom Stoppard*, Longman, Harlow, 1976.

CAHN, VICTOR: *Beyond Absurdity: The Plays of Tom Stoppard*, Fairleigh Dickinson University Press, New Jersey, 1979.

COHN, RUBY: 'Tom Stoppard: Light Drama and Dirges in Marriage', in *Contemporary English Drama*, ed. C. W. E. Bigsby, Edward Arnold, London, 1981, pp. 108–20.

DEAN, JOAN FITZPATRICK: *Tom Stoppard*, University of Missouri Press, Columbia and London, 1981.

HAYMAN, RONALD: *Tom Stoppard*, Heinemann Educational, London, 1977; third edition, 1979.

HAYMAN, RONALD: *Theatre and Anti-Theatre: New Movements since Beckett*, Secker & Warburg, London, 1979.

HUNTER, JIM: *Tom Stoppard's Plays*, Faber & Faber, London, 1982. Very much a practical guide to Stoppard's stagecraft; a book to use rather than one to read.

JAMES, CLIVE: 'Count Zero splits the Infinitive: Tom Stoppard's Plays', in *Encounter* (November 1975), 68–76. By a long way the best piece of criticism that Stoppard has so far elicited, but more difficult than its very funny introductory paragraphs might lead one to expect.

LONDRÉ, FELICIA HARDISON: *Tom Stoppard*, Frederick Ungar, New York, 1981. Some strained observations ('*Foot* . . . the part of the body most often mentioned in Stoppard's work') but includes a very useful *Chronology*.

MAROWITZ, CHARLES: *Confessions of a Counterfeit Critic: A London Theatre Notebook 1958–1971*, Eyre Methuen, London, 1973.

WHITAKER, THOMAS: *Fields of Play in Modern Drama*, Princeton University Press, Princeton, New Jersey, 1977.

The author of these notes

P. H. Parry was educated at the Universities of Bristol, Birmingham (The Shakespeare Institute), and St. Andrews, where he is now a lecturer in English Literature. He is the author of a volume on Wordsworth's poetry in the York Notes series.

York Notes: list of titles

CHINUA ACHEBE
A Man of the People
Arrow of God
Things Fall Apart

EDWARD ALBEE
Who's Afraid of Virginia Woolf?

ELECHI AMADI
The Concubine

ANONYMOUS
Beowulf
Everyman

JOHN ARDEN
Serjeant Musgrave's Dance

AYI KWEI ARMAH
The Beautyful Ones Are Not Yet Born

W. H. AUDEN
Selected Poems

JANE AUSTEN
Emma
Mansfield Park
Northanger Abbey
Persuasion
Pride and Prejudice
Sense and Sensibility

HONORÉ DE BALZAC
Le Père Goriot

SAMUEL BECKETT
Waiting for Godot

SAUL BELLOW
Henderson, The Rain King

ARNOLD BENNETT
Anna of the Five Towns

WILLIAM BLAKE
Songs of Innocence, Songs of Experience

ROBERT BOLT
A Man For All Seasons

ANNE BRONTË
The Tenant of Wildfell Hall

CHARLOTTE BRONTË
Jane Eyre

EMILY BRONTË
Wuthering Heights

ROBERT BROWNING
Men and Women

JOHN BUCHAN
The Thirty-Nine Steps

JOHN BUNYAN
The Pilgrim's Progress

BYRON
Selected Poems

ALBERT CAMUS
L'Etranger (The Outsider)

GEOFFREY CHAUCER
Prologue to the Canterbury Tales
The Franklin's Tale
The Knight's Tale
The Merchant's Tale
The Miller's Tale
The Nun's Priest's Tale
The Pardoner's Tale
The Wife of Bath's Tale
Troilus and Criseyde

ANTON CHEKHOV
The Cherry Orchard

SAMUEL TAYLOR COLERIDGE
Selected Poems

WILKIE COLLINS
The Moonstone
The Woman in White

SIR ARTHUR CONAN DOYLE
The Hound of the Baskervilles

WILLIAM CONGREVE
The Way of the World

JOSEPH CONRAD
Heart of Darkness
Lord Jim
Nostromo
The Secret Agent
Victory
Youth and *Typhoon*

STEPHEN CRANE
The Red Badge of Courage

BRUCE DAWE
Selected Poems

WALTER DE LA MARE
Selected Poems

DANIEL DEFOE
A Journal of the Plague Year
Moll Flanders
Robinson Crusoe

CHARLES DICKENS
A Tale of Two Cities
Bleak House
David Copperfield
Great Expectations
Hard Times
Little Dorrit
Nicholas Nickleby
Oliver Twist
Our Mutual Friend
The Pickwick Papers

EMILY DICKINSON
Selected Poems

JOHN DONNE
Selected Poems

THEODORE DREISER
Sister Carrie

GEORGE ELIOT
Adam Bede
Middlemarch
Silas Marner
The Mill on the Floss

T. S. ELIOT
Four Quartets
Murder in the Cathedral
Selected Poems
The Cocktail Party
The Waste Land

J. G. FARRELL
The Siege of Krishnapur

GEORGE FARQUHAR
The Beaux Stratagem

WILLIAM FAULKNER
Absalom, Absalom!
As I Lay Dying
Go Down, Moses
The Sound and the Fury

HENRY FIELDING
Joseph Andrews
Tom Jones

F. SCOTT FITZGERALD
Tender is the Night
The Great Gatsby

E. M. FORSTER
A Passage to India
Howards End

ATHOL FUGARD
Selected Plays

JOHN GALSWORTHY
Strife

MRS GASKELL
North and South

WILLIAM GOLDING
Lord of the Flies
The Inheritors
The Spire

OLIVER GOLDSMITH
She Stoops to Conquer
The Vicar of Wakefield

ROBERT GRAVES
Goodbye to All That

GRAHAM GREENE
Brighton Rock
The Heart of the Matter
The Power and the Glory

THOMAS HARDY
Far from the Madding Crowd
Jude the Obscure
Selected Poems
Tess of the D'Urbervilles
The Mayor of Casterbridge
The Return of the Native
The Trumpet Major
The Woodlanders
Under the Greenwood Tree

L. P. HARTLEY
The Go-Between
The Shrimp and the Anemone

NATHANIEL HAWTHORNE
The Scarlet Letter

SEAMUS HEANEY
Selected Poems

ERNEST HEMINGWAY
A Farewell to Arms
For Whom the Bell Tolls
The African Stories
The Old Man and the Sea

GEORGE HERBERT
Selected Poems

HERMANN HESSE
Steppenwolf

BARRY HINES
Kes

HOMER
The Iliad

ANTHONY HOPE
The Prisoner of Zenda

GERARD MANLEY HOPKINS
Selected Poems

WILLIAM DEAN HOWELLS
The Rise of Silas Lapham

RICHARD HUGHES
A High Wind in Jamaica

THOMAS HUGHES
Tom Brown's Schooldays

ALDOUS HUXLEY
Brave New World

HENRIK IBSEN
A Doll's House
Ghosts
Hedda Gabler

HENRY JAMES
Daisy Miller
The Europeans
The Portrait of a Lady
The Turn of the Screw
Washington Square

SAMUEL JOHNSON
Rasselas

BEN JONSON
The Alchemist
Volpone

JAMES JOYCE
A Portrait of the Artist as a Young Man
Dubliners

JOHN KEATS
Selected Poems

RUDYARD KIPLING
Kim

D. H. LAWRENCE
Sons and Lovers
The Rainbow
Women in Love

CAMARA LAYE
L'Enfant Noir

HARPER LEE
To Kill a Mocking-Bird

LAURIE LEE
Cider with Rosie

THOMAS MANN
Tonio Kröger

CHRISTOPHER MARLOWE
Doctor Faustus
Edward II

ANDREW MARVELL
Selected Poems

W. SOMERSET MAUGHAM
Of Human Bondage
Selected Short Stories

J. MEADE FALKNER
Moonfleet

HERMAN MELVILLE
Billy Budd
Moby Dick

THOMAS MIDDLETON
Women Beware Women

THOMAS MIDDLETON *and* WILLIAM ROWLEY
The Changeling

ARTHUR MILLER
Death of a Salesman
The Crucible

JOHN MILTON
Paradise Lost I & II
Paradise Lost IV & IX
Selected Poems

V. S. NAIPAUL
A House for Mr Biswas

SEAN O'CASEY
Juno and the Paycock
The Shadow of a Gunman

GABRIEL OKARA
The Voice

EUGENE O'NEILL
Mourning Becomes Electra

GEORGE ORWELL
Animal Farm
Nineteen Eighty-four

JOHN OSBORNE
Look Back in Anger

WILFRED OWEN
Selected Poems

ALAN PATON
Cry, The Beloved Country

THOMAS LOVE PEACOCK
Nightmare Abbey and *Crotchet Castle*

HAROLD PINTER
The Birthday Party
The Caretaker

PLATO
The Republic

ALEXANDER POPE
Selected Poems

THOMAS PYNCHON
The Crying of Lot 49

SIR WALTER SCOTT
Ivanhoe
Quentin Durward
The Heart of Midlothian
Waverley

PETER SHAFFER
The Royal Hunt of the Sun

WILLIAM SHAKESPEARE
A Midsummer Night's Dream
Antony and Cleopatra
As You Like It
Coriolanus
Cymbeline
Hamlet
Henry IV Part I
Henry IV Part II
Henry V
Julius Caesar
King Lear
Love's Labour's Lost
Macbeth
Measure for Measure
Much Ado About Nothing
Othello
Richard II
Richard III
Romeo and Juliet
Sonnets
The Merchant of Venice
The Taming of the Shrew
The Tempest
The Winter's Tale
Troilus and Cressida
Twelfth Night
The Two Gentlemen of Verona

GEORGE BERNARD SHAW
Androcles and the Lion
Arms and the Man
Caesar and Cleopatra
Candida
Major Barbara
Pygmalion
Saint Joan
The Devil's Disciple

MARY SHELLEY
Frankenstein

PERCY BYSSHE SHELLEY
Selected Poems

RICHARD BRINSLEY SHERIDAN
The School for Scandal
The Rivals

WOLE SOYINKA
The Lion and the Jewel
The Road
Three Short Plays

EDMUND SPENSER
The Faerie Queene (Book I)

JOHN STEINBECK
Of Mice and Men
The Grapes of Wrath
The Pearl

LAURENCE STERNE
A Sentimental Journey
Tristram Shandy

ROBERT LOUIS STEVENSON
Kidnapped
Treasure Island
Dr Jekyll and Mr Hyde

TOM STOPPARD
Professional Foul
Rosencrantz and Guildenstern are Dead

JONATHAN SWIFT
Gulliver's Travels

JOHN MILLINGTON SYNGE
The Playboy of the Western World

TENNYSON
Selected Poems

W. M. THACKERAY
Vanity Fair

DYLAN THOMAS
Under Milk Wood

EDWARD THOMAS
Selected Poems

FLORA THOMPSON
Lark Rise to Candleford

J. R. R. TOLKIEN
The Hobbit
The Lord of the Rings

CYRIL TOURNEUR
The Revenger's Tragedy

ANTHONY TROLLOPE
Barchester Towers

MARK TWAIN
Huckleberry Finn
Tom Sawyer

VIRGIL
The Aeneid

VOLTAIRE
Candide

EVELYN WAUGH
Decline and Fall
A Handful of Dust

JOHN WEBSTER
The Duchess of Malfi
The White Devil

H. G. WELLS
The History of Mr Polly
The Invisible Man
The War of the Worlds

ARNOLD WESKER
Chips with Everything
Roots

PATRICK WHITE
Voss

OSCAR WILDE
The Importance of Being Earnest

TENNESSEE WILLIAMS
The Glass Menagerie

VIRGINIA WOOLF
To the Lighthouse

WILLIAM WORDSWORTH
Selected Poems

W. B. YEATS
Selected Poems